Understanding MARIO VARGAS LLOSA

UNDERSTANDING MODERN EUROPEAN and LATIN AMERICAN LITERATURE

JAMES HARDIN, *SERIES EDITOR*

* * * * *

Understanding Günter Grass
by Alan Frank Keele

Understanding Graciliano Ramos
by Celso Lemos de Oliveira

Understanding Gabriel García Márquez
by Kathleen McNerney

Understanding Claude Simon
by Ralph Sarkonak

Understanding Mario Vargas Llosa
by Sara Castro-Klarén

UNDERSTANDING

MARIO VARGAS LLOSA

by SARA CASTRO-KLARÉN

UNIVERSITY OF SOUTH CAROLINA PRESS

Second Printing 1992

Published in Columbia, South Carolina, by the
University of South Carolina Press

Manufactured in the United States of America

Library of Congress Cataloging-in-Publication Data

Castro-Klarén, Sara.
Understanding Mario Vargas Llosa / by Sara Castro-Klarén.
p. cm.—(Understanding modern European and Latin American literature)
Includes bibliographical references.
ISBN 0-87249-668-6
ISBN 0-87249-848-4 (pbk)
1. Vargas Llosa, Mario, 1936– —Criticism and interpretation.
I. Title. II. Series.
PQ84898.32.A65Z644 1990
863—dc20 89-70449
CIP

Once again to Peter and Alexandra

CONTENTS

Editor's Preface **ix**

Acknowledgments **xi**

Chapter 1 Overview **1**

Chapter 2 *The Time of the Hero*: Machismo and No Exit **21**

Chapter 3 *The Green House*: Formal Experimentation and Marginal Territories **40**

Chapter 4 *Conversation in the Cathedral*: Descent into Hell **77**

Chapter 5 *The Perpetual Orgy* and Other Critical Writings: Self-Portrait of the Novelist **107**

Chapter 6 The Realm of Parody: Pantaleón and Aunt Julia **136**

Chapter 7 Cinematography and *The War of the End of the World* **163**

Chapter 8 Myth, Ideology, and Revolution: From Mayta to Tasurinchi **189**

Conclusion **224**

Select Bibliography **229**

Index **235**

EDITOR'S PREFACE

Understanding Modern European and Latin American Literature has been planned as a series of guides for undergraduate and graduate students and nonacademic readers. Like its companion series, *Understanding Contemporary American Literature,* the aim of the books is to provide an introduction to the life and writings of prominent modern authors and to explicate their most important works.

Modern literature makes special demands, and this is particularly true of foreign literature, in which the reader must contend not only with unfamiliar, often arcane artistic conventions and philosophical concepts, but also with the handicap of reading the literature in translation. It is a truism that the nuances of one language can be rendered in another only imperfectly (and this problem is especially difficult in fiction), but the fact that the works of European and Latin American writers are situated in historical and cultural settings quite different from our own can be as great a hindrance to the understanding of these works as the linguistic barrier. For this reason, the UMELL series will emphasize the sociological and historical background of the writers treated. The peculiar philosophical and cultural traditions of a given culture may be particularly important for an understanding of certain authors, and these will taken up in the introductory chapter and also in the discussion of those works to which this information is relevant. Beyond this, the books will treat the specifically literary aspects of the author under discussion and attempt to explain the complexities of contemporary literature lucidly. The books are conceived as introductions to the authors covered, not as comprehensive analyses. They do not provide detailed summaries of plot, as they are meant to be used in conjunction with the books they treat, not as a substitute for the study of the original works. It is our hope that the UMELL series will help to increase knowledge and understanding of the European and Latin American cultures and will serve to make the literature of those cultures more accessible.

Professor Castro-Klarén's *Understanding Mario Vargas Llosa* fills the need for an up-to-date study in English of one of the major figures of world literature today. And the book shows that discussion of literature, even "difficult" literature, can at the same time be lively and erudite.

J.H.

ACKNOWLEDGMENTS

I would like to express my gratitude to my students, to friends, and to colleagues for suggestive and valuable dialogue: Nicolás Wey, Max Hernández, Marta Paley, Luis Millones, Randolph Pope, Efraín Kristal, and Roberto Márquez. I especially thank here Dr. Everette Larson for the reference assistance he gave me at the Library of Congress. I also gratefully acknowledge the research funds made available by The John Hopkins University.

Understanding
MARIO VARGAS LLOSA

CHAPTER ONE

Overview

I

In the English-speaking world, and perhaps also in Europe, Mario Vargas Llosa is known as one of the major writers of what has been called the "boom" in Latin American literature. The other writers most often included in this phenomenon of stellar international prominence for Spanish American writers are Julio Cortázar, Jorge Luis Borges, Gabriel García Márquez, and Carlos Fuentes. But in specialized circles both the nature of the "boom" and the names of the writers included remain a topic of much debate. This is because the four writers named above are seen to represent only a limited sector of the broad and immensely rich variety of styles and themes cultivated by many other equally accomplished Spanish American writers. The weakness of the "boom" as a genuine phenomenon within Latin American literary history is made even more apparent by the consideration that the list of the four greats leaves out all of Brazilian literature. Nevertheless, the international critical success of Mario Vargas Llosa's novels is an indisputable fact, bolstered by the large number of languages into which his narratives have been quickly translated.[1]

Unlike many other Latin American writers in the past Mario Vargas Llosa has pursued, along with his development as a novelist, a prolific career as a journalist. And as a kind of journalist he has written extensively on literature, his own work, and contemporary political events. His reportage on the Cuban revolution, on the Sandinista revolution and on the struggle between capitalism and communism has been prominently featured in such influential American newspapers as the *New York Times*. In Europe his journalism has graced the influential pages of *Le Monde, The Times Literary Supplement,* and *El País*. He also writes for Latin American newspapers and magazines of wide continental circulation such as *Marcha* (Montevideo) and *Vuelta* (México). In short, his readership is international.

However, it would be a grave mistake to read Vargas Llosa's work—either his novels, his literary criticism, or his political journalism—outside the context of Latin American letters and history. Perhaps his own country's history is even more important to the understanding of novels such as *The War of the End of the World,* a story set in Brazil at the turn of the century; or even *The Perpetual Orgy,* an essay on the figurative father and son relation between two great storytellers: the French Gustave Flaubert and the Peruvian Mario Vargas Llosa.

In Vargas Llosa's early essays on the relationship of the writer to society the reader can easily see that he angrily explores the relationship of the rebellious young man to the Peruvian bourgeoisie of the 1950s. During the decade of the 50s Vargas Llosa had attended military school in Lima, completed high school in Piura, and entered San Marcos University in Lima. From 1948 to 1956 the country was under the grip of the military dictatorship of General Odría, which was often challenged by student and labor unrest. There can be little doubt that his direct experience with the military in the Leoncio Prado Military Academy and later at San Marcos University, which was riddled by the regime's spies (and under constant surveillance), indelibly marked Vargas Llosa's sense of freedom of the individual and its relationship to the state's power to restrict or annul it.

It was during this decade that Vargas Llosa found himself critically weighing his desire and inclination to write fiction and journalism. Judging from his essay on the Peruvian poet and playwright Sebastián Salazar Bondy and from his speech "Literature Is Fire,"[2] one can see that Vargas Llosa's view of the Peruvian writer's destiny was forged during the years of his literary studies at San Marcos. Although the decade of the 50s saw the "critical consecration" of José María Arguedas as the foremost national novelist,[3] it is clear that Vargas Llosa's affinity with the highly experimental and obscure Peruvian writers such as César Moro, Oquendo de Amat, and Martín Adán was a more important referent than Arguedas's experimentation with Quechua and the Andes. In fact, Vargas Llosa has written that he considered Arguedas's work an example of an old-fashioned regionalism that had already exhausted its imaginary possibilities.

The history of Peruvian literature is by no means devoid of great writers: Garcilaso de la Vega, El Inca, (1539–1616), José Carlos Mariátegui (1895–1930), César Vallejo (1892–1938), Martín Adán (pseudonym for Rafael de la Fuente Benavides, born in 1908), are all writers of international stature. Yet it is apparent that

Vargas Llosa does not regard their work as a principal influence on either his thought or his aesthetics. He has referred to his search for "something different" on several occasions. It seems that Vargas Llosa identified the Spanish American novel with what is known as the *novela de la tierra,* or Regionalist novel. Novels such as *Doña Bárbara* (1929 [*Doña Barbara,* 1931]) by the Venezuelan Rómulo Gallegos, *La vorágine* (1924 [*The Vortex,* 1935]) by José Eustasio Rivera of Colombia, or even *Los ríos profundos* by Arguedas stand in Vargas Llosa's mind as novels whose essential narrative flow is slowed down almost to a halt by lengthy descriptions of the land and treatises on rural life. While today there is a reappraisal of the *novela de la tierra*—and thus many a student of Latin American literature will disagree with Vargas Llosa's characterization of *Doña Bárbara* or *Los ríos profundos*—the fact remains that in the 1950s the young Peruvian was looking for a new and different novelistic form.

Vargas Llosa was in search of narrative structures and techniques that would enable him to portray his own contemporary, multifaceted experiences of urban Peru. The national life depicted in the Peru of his fiction is the life of a society caught in a furious process of urbanization. In this populous avalanche, as some sociologists have called it, many of the existing mental and material social structures entered a process of unremitting disintegration. This decay of the old order, in combination with the violence produced by the fear and loathing of the alienating and uncompromising unknown, stamps Vargas Llosa's fictional world with a terrifying sense of pain. Thus, he needed a narrative structure capable of encapsulating realistically, not the nostalgia for a beautiful though departing rural order, but rather the velocity of change in the everyday life of common individuals journeying from an unacceptable old order into the terrifying and relentless mixes of the cosmopolis. Lima may not strike many as a glamorous city in the sense that Paris, New York and Los Angeles have been portrayed by contemporary journalism. In terms of Peruvian history, however, the urban society emerging in Lima from the 1950s on is indeed cosmopolitan. For the first time in the four- or five-thousand year history of the Andean populations various ethnic groups from the four corners of the former Inca empire, and from the many social and racial layers created by Spanish colonial rule, came together in one urban center.

During the late 1950s and early 1960s the southern hemisphere's intellectual circles were rocked by the work of Jean-Paul Sartre. Existentialism, with its denial of God and essence of being, fell on fertile ground. Even more important than the denial of God as the ultimate referent for life's meaning was existentialism's redefinition of being as merely the flux and sum total of existence. The existentialists' affirmation of human and secular contingency took root and developed in the furrow of an old and vigorous anticlericalism characteristic of Latin America's educated youth. Although perhaps only a few actually understood the complexity of *L'Être et le néant* (1943 [*Being and Nothingness,* 1956]), Sartre's Existentialism, like Marxism before and after World War II, could be reduced to a set of easily digestible tenets. Existentialism's assertions that man's freedom is inevitable took on an immediate and local political import within the Latin

American context. Sartre's call to authenticity, to confrontation with the powers that be, and his commitment to moral and political engagement were, of course, not lost on the university student who knew his generation caught in the grip of a dictatorship or a fossilized society that resisted all change. University students of the 1950s regarded themselves as yet another new generation eager to find untried horizons within which they could define their generational historical project.

The translation into Spanish in 1950 of *Qu'est-ce-que la littérature?* (1947 [*What Is Literature?*, 1949]) was an epoch-making intellectual event in Spanish America. Vargas Llosa credits Sartre with having opened for him the windows to a horizon of creative freedom that the young writer had longed for but could not find in his own surroundings. The Sartre that Vargas Llosa refers to, I believe, is not the philosopher, but the playwright of *Huis clos* (1944 [*No Exit,* 1947]) and *Les mouches* (1943 [*The Flies,* 1947]), and especially the existentialist novelist of *Le sursis* (1945 [*The Reprieve,* 1947]) and *Le mur* (1939 [*The Wall,* 1947]). Sartre's narratives pointed the way to the technical innovations for which Vargas Llosa was searching. For instance, Vargas Llosa's extensive use of conversation as the chief format for his major three early novels is unmistakably affiliated with Sartre's technique in his wartime novel, *The Reprieve.*

The Vargas Llosa of *La casa verde* (1965 [*The Green House,* 1968]) has, in several of the many interviews he has given, indicated that his early encounter with the French masters was probably decisive in his formation as a creative writer. As a child Vargas Llosa was an enthralled reader of Alexander Dumas and Victor Hugo. Later on in Lima, during his college days, he worked at the library of the Club Nacional, a stodgy aristocratic institution in which the males of the Peruvian bourgeoisie played at being members of a traditional upper-class British club. The Club Nacional apparently subscribed to several French journals and also had a rather good collection of French piquant, erotic, and even pornographic novels. Restif de la Breton, Émile Zola, Gustave Flaubert, and even the Marquis de Sade seem to have been well represented in this rather select library. Along with Sartre's political philosophy this other branch of French thought and culture offered Vargas Llosa a broad canvas on which sensitivities and sensibilities often considered forbidden in Peru's narrow, middle-class, Catholic culture were explored in subtle, morose, violent, and pleasure-filled detail. And so it is not surprising that Vargas Llosa should claim Gustave Flaubert to have been the major influence on his novelistic craft. Honoring, acknowledging, and nourishing the filial or brotherly relations with Flaubert, Vargas Llosa wrote *La Orgía perpetua, Flaubert y Madame Bovary* (1975 [*The Perpetual Orgy,* 1986]).

It would seem that while Vargas Llosa read widely during his formative years, the years when he struggled with the composition of *La ciudad y los perros* (1963 [*The time of the Hero,* 1966]) and *The Green House,* he discriminated among the elements that he pursued for the creation of a novelistic style that he could consider his own and discarded others equally available to him. During the early part of the decade of the 60s Vargas Llosa was living and working in

Paris. The French lessons that he had taken in Lima came in handy, and although his French was foreign-sounding to Parisian ears, he nevertheless found a job broadcasting programs in Spanish at the Radio-Television Française. This part-time job left him enough leisure to read and write.

Paris was then enamored with the *nouveau roman* (the New Novel). Alain Robbe-Grillet and his revolutionary attack on realism, as well as on allegory, symbol, and "depth" in *Pour un nouveau roman* (1963 [*For a New Novel,* 1965]), set the pace of artistic and intellectual circles in Paris. Perched in his tiny suite in the attic of a Parisian apartment house, Vargas Llosa noted the main tenets of the *nouveau roman* and rejected them. He wanted to tell stories, and would hold to his preference for the action novel and the broad canvas. He did, however, pay keen attention to William Faulkner and Ernest Hemingway, for their novelistic strategies offered solutions to problems that he himself was confronting in the telling of action-packed, multifaceted stories.

Given his close connection to the nineteenth-century French masters and his own firm sense of affinities, it is not surprising that Vargas Llosa should situate his own work at a distance from any Spanish American or even Spanish predecessor. Cervantes, considered by Flaubert to be the father of the modern novel, is hardly ever mentioned by Vargas Llosa. The closest to anything proceeding from the Iberian peninsula was his enthusiasm for a forgotten Catalonian writer of a late medieval chivalric novel: *Tirant lo Blanc* (1490). Such a distance from the Iberian peninsula is not at all peculiar to Vargas Llosa or to other Spanish American writers. Rather, it is symptomatic of Latin American literature in its quest for originality, for authentic historical representation, and for modernity.

II

When Mario Vargas Llosa left Peru for Europe in 1959, he had barely finished the equivalent of a bachelor's degree with a major in literature, which at San Marcos University meant mostly Spanish and Peruvian literature, just as an English major in the United States includes mostly English and American literature. He was by then married to Julia Urquidi, an aunt. At the age of nineteen Vargas Llosa fell passionately in love with a divorcée more than ten years his elder. She was the sister of his maternal uncle's wife. The young and attractive divorcée had come to visit her sister in Lima, and the Llosa family thought that the young man Marito could amuse the family's guest. One thing led to another, and one day, against the wishes of the entire family and the father's death threat, Marito and Julia eloped. Even though he held a variety of part-time jobs—journalist, news broadcaster, cemetery guardian, librarian—he was basically unemployed. His eminent history professor and friend, Raúl Porras Barrenechea, helped him get a scholarship to pursue his literary studies in Spain. But Vargas Llosa's destination was never really Madrid. The object of his desire was Paris, a city that he had briefly visited a year before when he won the Revue Française Prize (1958) for his short story "El desafio." While in Madrid he attended classes that bored him to death. He spent the bulk of his time reading, writing, and having a good time meeting and enjoying the company of many other Spanish and Latin American young men who also aspired to an artistic or intellectual career.

The year of the scholarship soon came to an end. The young writer had more or less finished a version of the novel he was working on, but he was still not satisfied with it. Its intended title was *La morada del héroe* (The Hero's Dwelling), and it dealt partly with his recollections of the days he had lived in the Leoncio Prado Military Academy. Faced with the possibility of returning to Peru, he and his wife decided to resettle in Paris.

This first year in Spain and the subsequent years he was to live in Paris, London, and Barcelona proved to be a period of enormous creativity. Some people refer to this time spent in Europe as Vargas Llosa's exile, but such a term could be confusing in his case, for he had voluntarily left his country and chosen to stay abroad for reasons of his own. The Peruvian government has actually never placed any prohibition on Vargas Llosa's choice of residence or the range of his political activity.

Once settled in Paris, the young writer set out once again with the strongest determination to rewrite *La morada del héroe,* which at times was also titled *Los impostores* (The Impostors). A chance meeting with Carlos Barral, the co-owner of one of the most powerful Spanish publishing houses, provided the place for submission of the manuscript. Barral submitted the novel for consideration for the Premio Biblioteca Breve, Spain's most prestigious literary prize, and Vargas Llosa's tale about a handful of terrified and terrifying adolescents won, by unanimous vote, first prize in

1963. The novel, by then retitled *La ciudad y los perros* (*The Time of the Hero,* 1966), was the first ever to win the Biblioteca Breve prize for a Latin American writer. It launched Vargas Llosa's fortunes into an international market and a path of success which he has maintained with the publication of each of his successive novels.

Although *The Time of the Hero* is Vargas Llosa's first novel, the technical skill, daring, and innovation displayed in the telling of the story was so captivating that it became the focus of critical praise and attention. The separate and, at the same time, integrated story of the Circle boys is narrated in distinct cinematic fashion. It relies on the swift combination of short scenes, each narrated from a multiplicity of points of view. In contrast with the long background description and characterization of the established realistic narrative, *The Time of the Hero* progresses at great speed by means of the cinematic "take and cut" assemblage procedure. Introductions are avoided. The ending of each scene is barely suggested before the next image is already full-blown in the reader's consciousness. An avalanche of images superimposed on each other evolves at enormous speed, without allowing time for all the links to be spelled out. This mode of narration was totally new in Spanish America, and it won the novel an immediate place among distinguished contemporary novels.

The Time of the Hero told the story of a group of adolescents confined in a military academy at the time of passage into adulthood. *La casa verde,* 1966 (*The Green House)* found its setting in the sprawling and fragmented territory of northern Peru. In their adventures the characters of *The Green House* respond, like the characters of *The Time of the Hero,* to two sets of names, depending on a given social milieu. They also move between the jungle and the desert, between Brazil and Peru, between forgotten provincial outposts and Lima, the center of power in Peruvian life. The set of double names for chief characters such as Bonifacia/Selvática indicates an irreparable but often ambiguous break in the life and person of such characters. Such rupture in characters' names also affects the continuity of the narrative. In *The Green House,* Vargas Llosa tells, with shifting and contrasting points of view, the riveting stories of some thirty-four characters, all in search of a niche that will enable them to lead mediocre, peaceful lives. The only character who seems to have achieved such privilege is Aquilino, the kind and wise old boatman who is compassionate enough to take Fushía downriver to his last destination, the leprosorium.

While the autobiographical elements are very few in *The Green House,* with the two-volume *Conversación en La Catedral* (1969 [*Conversation in the Cathedral,* 1975]), Vargas Llosa returns fully to the scenes of his early years in Peru. *The Time of the Hero* depicts the painful memory of the puzzling and alienating days spent in the Leoncio Prado Military Academy. This suffocating atmosphere of hypocrisy and cynicism reappears in all its power in *Conversation in The Cathedral,* a novel that delves into the college days of Zavalita, the rebel-would-be-hero son of a well-to-do family. The entire time of the novel is framed within the four-hour conversation, or dual reminiscence, held between Zavalita—now a journalist—and his father's former chauffeur—now a dogcatcher and executioner whose job is to club dogs to death in the pound. Lima lives now under the torpor of civilian rule. The life experience evoked by the two men's memory brings back the oppressive days of the Odría dictatorship and the student-worker failed struggle against his machine of corruption. In this profoundly pessimistic novel, considered by many to be Vargas Llosa's best, the author of so many experimental techniques hones his use of conversation as a narrative device to its highest and most precise level.

Vargas Llosa's publications on literature—his own and books written by writers whom he admires—deserve separate space and will be discussed in chapter 5. Suffice it to say here that his commentary on the medieval novel *Tirant lo Blanc;* his reflections on his own making of *The Green House, La historia secreta de una novela* (1971 [A Novel's Secret Story]); and his doctoral dissertation *García Márquez: Historia de un deicidio* (1971 [García Márquez: Story of a Deicide]), have appeared in book form. This body of critical commentary is quite important, not only for the understanding of Vargas Llosa's views about literature and society, the novel in general, and his own craft, but also because it has proven to be highly influential on those who have written on his work.

With *Pantaleón y las visitadoras* (1973 [*Captain Pantoja and the Special Service,* 1978]) Vargas Llosa surprised most of his readers, delighted a good many, and puzzled quite a few others. After the sadness and gloom of *Conversation in The Cathedral,* the crude and cruel humor of *Captain Pantoja* was, if nothing else, a new departure. Like *The Green House,* this novel is set in the jungle, with brief forays to Lima and the northern provincial town of Chiclayo. The army, its self-serving spirit, and its blinding combination of arrogance and insecurity constitute the target for Vargas Llosa's humor in this novel. Pantaleón Pantoja's story, which Vargas Llosa says he heard on one of his trips to Iquitos or Pucallpa, is the story of a well-meaning, disciplined, efficient, simple bureaucrat whose very qualities turn him into a ridiculous monster when, in his passion to accomplish his secret mission, he devises the most "scientifically" efficient means of providing the socially starved troops with "maximum opportunities of sexual gratification." The novels' plot and humor are in this way reminiscent of some Hollywood movies about army life in remote outposts of the tropical Pacific and the efforts of an enterprising, low-level officer to liven up the dull scene with local girls and/or contraband liquor (Marlon Brando as the Oriental procurer for Glenn Ford, who in turn plays the reformist but eventually corrupted officer in *Tea House of the August Moon* [1956]; Ernest Borgnine and Tim Conway in *McHale's Navy;* the Captain in *Gilligan's Island).*

In 1966 Vargas Llosa codirected a film version of *Captain Pantoja.* It was shot in the Dominican Republic and shown with good commercial success throughout Latin America. In this film the provocative and even *tremendista* (extremely truculent) sexual aspects of the novel were emphasized over the satire directed at the military bureaucracy. The film was, in short, reminiscent of the gross musical made in pre-revolutionary Cuba in which María Antonieta Pons, a mambo dancer, dances her robust body to stardom.

In 1977 Vargas Llosa returned to Lima and to his own life with *La tía Julia y el escribidor* [*Aunt Julia and the Scriptwriter,* 1982]. This time the shadows are gone, the mood is light, characters meet and visit places in full daylight. *Aunt Julia,* more so than *Captain Pantoja,* is a novel that parodies itself, the act of narration, the craft of the writer, and above all the sentimentality of love prevalent in soap-opera versions of life. The novel tells the story of a struggling young man who aspires to be a writer. In the space of roughly one year Marito despairs at becoming a full-time professional writer. His best model, Camacho, after maddening success, suffers a mental breakdown after the demand for him to produce scatological and apocalyptic plots proves to be too great. Unwittingly the scriptwriter begins to confuse the separate plot lines of the several radio soap operas he is simultaneously writing. In his derangement he kills the wrong characters, resurrects the bad guys, and rewards the wrong people. Finally, his public rebels, and Marito is asked by the owners of the radio station to salvage what is left of the intertwined plots. In the meantime Marito has been weaving a strange plot of his own. He has fallen in love with a much older woman, who also happens to be the sister of his uncle's wife. Not related by blood, Marito and Julia decide to get married, even though they know that the entire family will not only object but actually use any means necessary to prevent the couple's incestuous plans. Marito's farcical race to the altar in a hot and forgotten fishing village in the Peruvian desert would seem right out of Camacho's own plot repertoire. Read at this level, the novel offers an easy and most enjoyable reading experience, especially for the non-Latin American reader. At another level the plots of the novel are charged with social issues that Vargas Llosa had been exploring before *Aunt Julia and the Scriptwriter,* and would continue to examine in subsequent novels.

Just before the publication of another long and great novel, *La guerra del fin del mundo* (1981 [*The War of the End of the World,* 1984]), Vargas Llosa published his first play, *La señorita de Tacna* (The Young Lady from Tacna), with which he won the Annual Critic's Award in Argentina. The monumental achievement that *The War of the End of the World* represents eclipsed the fact that Vargas Llosa had moved into yet another genre, the theater. However, within the general context of his work this theatrical venture is not at all disassociated from the manner in which he constructs and moves characters, and much less from the extensive use of dialogue, conversation, and stream of consciousness that he employs in his narrative. In fact, *The War of the End of the World* had a previous version as a movie script that was never filmed.

Two elements are entirely new in *The War of the End of the World.* First, it is a historical novel, a tale about events that actually took place during the last decade of the nineteenth century in northeastern Brazil. Second, Vargas Llosa's novel is faithfully based on the earlier Brazilian classic *Os Sertões* (1902 [*Rebellion in the Backlands,* 1944]), written by Euclides da Cunha. The fictional version of the events of Canudos is depicted on an enormous canvas. Its epic quality is overpowering—in fact, it is reminiscent of the great Hollywood films dealing with episodes from the Old Testament, Roman life, or the Crusades. Like *Exodus,*

Quo Vadis?, *The Centurion,* and others, *The War of the End of the World* moves masses of people on a pilgrimage over a vast and hostile territory until the crucial place for the final battle is reached. Friends and enemies are moved by a religious or quasi-religious spirit, and the impending fight to death is written in the air they breathe, the rags they wear, and the passion that holds them together and moves them to kill in self-defense. The power of the story of the Counselor and his followers displaces the previous emphasis on dazzling technique. The Counselor is a mystic and passionate believer in Christ's evangelical message of love amongst the poor and promise of the kingdom of heaven. His tragic confrontation with the Brazilian army is portrayed with the vivid plastic force of film. The war in Canudos is bloody and morbid. This novel's emphasis on sheer action makes it in may ways reminiscent of the battle scenes in *War and Peace* and *The Three Musketeers.*

Following *The War of the End of the World,* and before the publication of his most recent three novels, Vargas Llosa wrote another play, *Kathie y el hipopótamo* (1933 [Kathie and the Hippopotamus]). This curious play delves into the melodramatic fantasy of a woman without a past worth memorializing. Her desire to have memories worth recounting—adventures—leads her to hire a journalist, Zavalita, to act as a ghostwriter for her nonexistent autobiography. Zavalita writes down her fantasized trip to Africa.

With *Historia de Mayta* (1984 [*The Real Life of Alejandro Mayta,* 1986]), Vargas Llosa created another controversy among many of his readers. In this novel the narrator directly informs the reader that he is the famous Peruvian writer Mario Vargas Llosa. The task he has set for himself in this book is to write the biography of a forgotten and failed revolutionary by the name of Alejandro Mayta. The novel pretends to delve into the anatomy, if not of revolution, at least of the revolutionary man. As the narrator investigates Mayta's past, the portrait of a sensitive, compassionate, lower-middle-class young man emerges clearly. The narrator attempts to link early Catholic sensitivities and convictions of solidarity with one's suffering fellowman with an unexplained and sudden conversion to communism. Although Vargas Llosa has argued that the book's main purpose is the examination of the writer's métier as a creator of believable realities, in many quarters the novel was read as an ideological attempt to discredit the left and its participation in the political process in Latin America. Mayta, the Trotskyite, expelled from almost every organized, splintered, leftist party, in conspiracy with a lieutenant in the army, concocts a revolutionary uprising in Jauja, a rather remote province in the northern Peruvian Andes. The fact that only Mayta, his coconspirator, and a few high school students show up at zero hour is taken in the novel as the best proof that the scheme is harebrained. As in *Conversation in The Cathedral,* the relationship of Mayta's story to actual events in recent Peruvian political history is clear to Vargas Llosa's contemporaries. In fact, while the foreign reader can easily follow the plot and its logic without any knowledge of Peruvian or Latin American politics, many an educated Peruvian or Latin American can read *The Real Story of Alejandro Mayta* as a *roman á clef,* or a direct commentary on the political struggle of the last quarter century in Latin America.

Vargas Llosa repeatedly chooses three distinct geographic and social spaces from the large variety of Peruvian regions as the settings for his novels. For his early short stories, *Los jefes* (1959 [*The Cubs and Other Stories,* 1978]), and many of his novels Lima is the historical space that the narrative articulates. *The Green House* oscillates between the jungle and the provincial coastal town of Piura. With *¿Quién mató a Palomino Molero?* (1986 [*Who Killed Palomino Molero?* 1987]), Vargas Llosa returns to Piura and also to the 1950s, the decade in Peruvian life when most of his plots take place.

In this relatively short novel Vargas Llosa makes full use of the detective novel format. From the very beginning the task of the reader becomes the discovery of the motives and the identity of Molero's murderer(s). As in most of his previous novels, the characters here function mostly as vehicles for the plot. The armed forces, this time the more openly racist and classist air force, appear pitted against, but also in alliance with, the civilian society in the nearby towns. Molero's murder is depicted in its full brutality. It seems that, under orders from a white lieutenant, a group of soldiers kidnap and murder the unemployed, guitar-playing lower-class Molero. His crime is to have fallen in love with and seduced the colonel's daughter, whose marriage to the lieutenant had been, of course, prearranged. *Who Killed Palomino Molero?* has not met with the critical acclaim accorded to the rest of Vargas Llosa's novels. In fact, it is considered his weakest novel.

In another great incursion into the jungle and into the new society that the violent intrusion of contemporary social forces is inflicting upon the original inhabitants of the Amazon Basin, Vargas Llosa has written his most recent mythic tale of violence. With *El hablador* (1987 [*The Storyteller*, 1989]), a book that, like *The War of the End of the World* and *The Green House,* required several years of research and numerous trips to the area of its geographical setting, Vargas Llosa embarks on the disclosure of a rarely touched aspect of the human condition. *El Hablador* will not close the enormous cycle of novels that this prolific and genial writer has given his public. At barely fifty-five he is, as novelists go, still young. The eventual quantity and richness of his production could indeed reach and rival that of Honoré de Balzac, one of the French classic writers that he most admires.

NOTES

1. To date, Mario Vargas Llosa's novels have been translated into almost all European languages, as well as Japanese and Chinese.

2. Mario Vargas Llosa, "La literatura es fuego," *Contra viento y marea* (Barcelona: Seix Barral, 1983).

3. José María Arguedas, author of several major novels including *Todas las sangres* (1964) and *El zorro de arriba y el zorro de abajo* (1971), rose to prominence in 1958 with the publication of his epochmaking, semiautobiographical novel, *Los ríos profundos* (translated as *Deep Rivers* [Austin: University of Texas Press, 1978]).

CHAPTER TWO

The Time of the Hero: Machismo and No Exit

Vargas Llosa's literary production begins with the publication in 1957 of his first short stories, "Los jefes" (The Leaders) and "El abuelo" (The Grandfather), in two different newspapers in Lima (*El Mercurio Peruano* and *El Comercio,* respectively). Almost ten years later he published *Los cachorros* (1967 [*The Cubs and Others Stories,* 1979]), a collection of stories that includes the short novel *Los cachorros* and some of the short stories included earlier in *Los jefes,* 1959. The short stories, together with the novella, are seen now as narratives containing the kernels of what later evolved into the chief themes not only of *The time of the Hero* but actually of his entire fictional world; violence in an endless complex of modulations, hatred, alienation, perversion, corruption, betrayal, lying, treason, deceit, injustice, murder, and machismo. This myriad portrayal of violence is set forth in a dazzling experimentation with narrative rhetoric.

In "Los jefes," as well as in *Los cachorros* and *The Time of the Hero,* the story centers on the agonizing crossing of boys into manhood. As the boys leave home—the realm of the mother—they must make their way to the shores of the adult world, that is, to the privileged site of machismo. Alberto, Pichula,

Miguel, Rubén, and Boa, must all learn to win in the game of dissimulation and perversion. Nothing seems acceptable except the mask of indifference before pain. Defiance of the established power goes hand in hand with the readiness for hypocritical pacts of convenience between those who represent authority and those who challenge it. In retrospect Vargas Llosa affirms that he believes that, in the society he depicts, violence is at the root of all human relations. Violence anchors the world of his adolescent characters. It is manifest in all gestures and actions of normal daily life, itself portrayed as a series of betrayals, corporeal abuse, verbal terror, and sometimes death and even murder.

In "Los jefes," "El desafio" (The Challenge), "Día Domingo" (On Sunday), "El hermano menor" (The Younger Brother), "Un visitante" (A Visitor), and "El abuelo" (The Grandfather), the civilian society of Miraflores and Bellavista of *The Time of the Hero* appears already delineated in its major characteristics. A domestic female world appears, populated by soft, submissive, superficial women who "suffer" the relationship by which they are attached to a more or less macho male. The world of the males, constantly tensed up by an ever-present challenge inscribed in all their relationships, even when they appear to be a solidaristic group, turns the entire social fabric into an alienating environment in which mutilation and murderous violence can erupt at any moment.

In the tighter space of the short story Vargas Llosa generally pits two individuals against each other. The conflict that ensues produces a domino-like effect on the rest of the characters in the story. This inevitable deterministic effect is like the opening of *The Time of the Hero.* In that scene, after Cava rolls the fatidic number four, the rest of the story proceeds inevitably to its conclusion.

A Simple Tale with an Ambiguous End

Reduced to the bare essentials of the action, the plot of *The Time of the Hero* seems rather simple and straightforward. Gathered in a dark and dingy bathroom at the Leoncio Prado Military Academy, four cadets known as "The Circle" throw dice in order to draw lots and choose the individual who will steal a copy of the chemistry examination scheduled for the next day. Cava draws number four. He steals the examination according to Jaguar's plan, but accidentally breaks a glass pane in the window of the classroom. The noise alerts one of the boys assigned to patrol that night. Although Slave does not stop Cava, he does see him. When the theft of the exam is discovered by the military officers who run the school, the entire school is punished. There is no relief from the punishment until the truth is revealed. Under the pressure of the severe punishment—no one can go home for weekends—a cadet secretly comes forward and reveals the identity of the thief and the existence of the Circle. While the obligatory investigation is being carried out, the cadets go away on maneuvers. Slave is mysteriously shot in the head and killed. Alberto, known as the Poet, accuses Jaguar of the murder.

Because of fear for the Poet's safety, he is placed in jail. Jaguar, accused of murder, is also jailed while the investigation continues. Jaguar insists not only on his innocence but on the notion that even if he knew, he would not tell because of his spirit of loyalty toward his fellow cadets. This he calls his code of honor. He feels infinitely superior to the Poet. When the investigation is completed and the colonel who runs the school is supposed to be in possession of all the scandalous and terrifying facts put forth before the reader in the course of the novel, a cover-up ensues. Jaguar is set free, the Poet is made to retract his accusations, and the whole incident is officially declared a deplorable accident. The action of the novel takes place in roughly a two-month period.

The action of the plot weaves a thread through the key points in the texture of the crisis. The deeper colors in this tapestry of terror and excitement are portrayed in the moments when each boy's past is told in conjunction with his fantasies. Memory and desire are interrelated throughout the novel. Such a play between a past seen through the prism of nostalgia—the boys know that the days of innocence are gone—and the immediate future as the realm of desire fulfilled gives the characters of the boys a depth not often achieved by Vargas Llosa in his later novels.

Multiple Point of View and Density

The structure of the novel emerges out of the organizational relations established among a series of fragments. The story line is fragmented. The reading sequence does not coincide with the actual sequence of events that constitute the plot. Each character is presented by means of an endlessly fragmented point of view.

Mechanically the novel is divided into eight chapters and an epilogue. Each chapter in turn is broken down into short segments. Three long scenes make up the epilogue. The entire novel contains a total of eighty-two movable segments that alternate between the past and the present, between the military academy and the city, between the cadets and the neighborhood friends, between family life and the all-male world of the school, between the social codes at Leoncio Prado Academy and the social norms of the civilian world, and especially between the viewpoints of one or another of the several narrators. Each segment can, at any given moment, represent a combination of any number of the alternatives listed above, giving the novel a kaleidoscopic quality in which new multiple combinations seem always possible.

Although there are many different combinations of point of view, narrator's identity, and locales, the scenes given in each segment seem to alternate between the past and present. This movement marks a basic beat or rhythm. The overall forward movement of the narrative rests on a contrapuntal feeling, on a sense of duality that eventually lends the novel its density. The constant interaction of the fragments, in particular the constant sway between the ever-present time of interior monologue and personal point of view, creates an overwhelming sense of simultaneity for the entire novel. In no way is Vargas Llosa's break from the mimetic conventions of nineteenth-century realism more clearly accomplished than in this achievement of simultaneity that ultimately blurs our sense of linear chronology.

A brief description of the narrative elements combined in the five segments that make up chapter 3 gives us a good idea of Vargas Llosa's novelistic technique and world. The opening of the chapter is set in the mystery and contradiction of a narrator who directly speaks to the reader in the first person but whose identity remains uncertain. The reminiscent voice states:

> I was then enrolled in the Sáenz Peña school. I would walk home, to Bellavista. Sometimes I would run into Higueras. He was one of my brother's friends before Perico got drafted into the Army. He would always ask: "What have you heard from him?"
>
> "Nothing. Since he was posted to the jungle, he has not written."
>
> He would take me to a bar. The pisco burned my throat and made my eyes water. "Suck on a piece of lime," he would say, "it is smoother that way. And smoke a cigarette"[1](63).

It is only at the end of the novel that we are given enough of the right clues to realize that the unidentified narrator of this poignant recollection is actually Jaguar. In this segment of chapter 3 the boy tenderly chronicles his loneliness, his sweet puppy love for his next-door neighbor Teresa, and the "natural" and friendly way in which his brother's friend, Higueras, initiated him into drinking, smoking, deceitfulness, and even callousness—all virtues that will serve him well on the way to the top, as head of The Circle, once he enters the military academy. At the end the narrator of the segment stresses his sense of deprivation. He and his mother had barely enough money to pay for rent and food. That year, he recalls, he did not go to the movies at all. Next year, in contrast, even though he had plenty of money, he was always bitter, especially when he began to reminisce about the afternoons when he and Teresa did their homework together.

The segments narrated by the anonymous voice abruptly end, followed by another segment in which the narrator takes up the subject of films subtly brought up at the end of the previous segment. "But movies were even better than the chicken or the midget. Take it easy Skimpy, I can even feel your teeth." The mention of the chicken is the clue that tells us that the voice no longer belongs to the narrator of the first segment. We are here in the presence of Boa, his chicken, his dog, and his sexual pleasures. Boa's reminiscence is this time not about his own past or present. It is in fact a portrayal of Jaguar and of his abilities as a leader, a terrorist, and a *caudillo*. Boa sets the scene for the free-for-all boxing match that Jaguar provokes at the cinema to avenge himself on the graduating cadets. A posteriori, Boa comments:

> And it was even better than before, because when we were Dogs, The Circle counted only for our section, but this time it was as if the entire second-year class was identified with The Circle and we were the ones who actually gave the orders and of course Jaguar was in command even more than the rest of us in The Circle (65).

Vargas Llosa's dovetailing technique is flawless. Even though the shift from one segment to the next seems abrupt, inasmuch as there is always a major shift in narrator, point of view, locale, and events, the author is always careful to have some very clear though subliminal marks to provide continuity. Between the two disparate segments he uses the reference to the movies and the name of the objects of attachment of two narrators: Tere for Jaguar, and Skimpy for Boa. These elements for dovetailing are, of course, supportive of the fact that the two segments complement each other in the portrayal of Jaguar. In the first segment we are given a sad, sweet recollection of a young boy, his friends, and neighborhood. In contrast, in Boa's segment, the novel presents a scene of swift, tumultuous action and gross humor in which Jaguar appears garbed in his full armor of defiance, courage, and cynicism:

> There was a war. It was clear with the movies incident and also with the business of the rape. . . .
>
> "Don't you want to obey?" said the graduating cadet.
>
> "No," said Jaguar, "why should I?" . . . He was having fun baiting him. . . . It is going to happen, and in the dark. . . . Everyone stood up and I saw the shadows all over me. They begun kicking me. I don't remember a thing about the movie. And what about the Poet? They were really creaming him, or was he just pretending with all that screaming. . . . And the Dogs began shouting, "Lights, lights!" The air was full of cigarettes, everyone wanted to get rid of them, we were not about to get caught smoking. It was a miracle there was not a fire. What a fight, come on, boys, let them have it, the moment for our revenge is here! (66–67).

In Boa's reminiscence the past is brought back to the present of the narrator's enunciation, so that the dialogues seem to occur in the same present as the reader's reading present. Boa's recollection is so vivid in his affective memory that he often substitutes the past for the present tense in his narrative. "It was a miracle there was not a fire" is immediately followed by a call to arms in the present: "Come on, boys, let them have it!" This, in turn, is followed by another statement in the past tense: "What beasts, they began throwing out blows in all directions. How could I forget it, Rat gave me a direct hit in the chest, he knocked the wind out of me" (67–68).

Boa's recollection opens the way, again thematically, for Alberto's segment. Unforgettable to Boa is the lesson in self-defense and group solidarity taught by Jaguar after the boxing match. Expecting yet another cycle of revenge and dissimulation, Boa reflects: "And later, what a masquerade! Everything is O.K., we are all friends.... But we knew we had to defend ourselves, ... stick shaving blades in the tips of your shoes; fill your pockets with rocks" (68). In the third segment, in a milder way, a semiomniscient voice, another narrator, adopting Alberto's point of view, draws scene after scene, delving into the dynamics of group formation in Alberto's two-block neighborhood. Just as in the military academy, rivals face down each other until one, Alberto, emerges as the undisputed leader of the pack. Alberto, known as the Poet at the academy, is shown running at the head of the pack of players, running away from the scene of the crime (a broken window). Among Pluto, Tico, Bebe, Emilio, Paco, and Sorbino, Alberto emerges as the passionate but diplomatic strategist of the descent from the city to the beach: "He would point to the details of the descent with short phrases, imitating the gestures and body language of heroes in the movies. . . . They moved down slowly, enveloped in a deep sense of fraternity" (70–71). Alberto's middle-class group experiences here a sense of solidarity, a good feeling not unlike the feeling of elation and common purpose that Boa tried to evoke in his recollection of the fight at the movies and the track-and-field meet at the military academy.

The fourth segment is Boa's once more. Here he recalls the humiliation that Jaguar's extended circle of defiance perpetrated on the officers of the academy when the boys went out of their way to win the rope-pulling contest, earlier alluded to in Boa's recollection of the episode at the movies. Again Boa narrates in a stream-of-consciousness style, assuming as given the social world of the entire story, avoiding description, and mixing the present time of his recollections with the past of the "actual" fictive present.

Boa's recollection of the track and field competition ends on a serious reflective note. For him life in the academy is tough, but things could be worse. Indeed, it would be much worse if they were to be expelled because of Cava. The mention of Cava provides a bridge to the current time and action of the plot: the theft of the exam, which in itself is a coded bridge to Richi, or Slave, the boy who was on patrol duty the night that Cava went out to steal the exam.

Richi's segment, like Alberto's, is told in the voice of a semiomniscient narrator whose omniscience is limited because he adopts Richi's point of view as his own vantage point in the world. This episode explores Richi's depressed state of mind when his mother is reunited with his father, a stern and severe man whom the boy fears. Like Jaguar's and Alberto's memories, Richi's consciousness focuses on the bittersweet routines of a world shattered forever with the onset of manhood. This segment, unlike Alberto's, is more keenly focused on Richi's interiority, on his feelings of rejection, on his own image as reflected in his father's and mother's conversations about him or with him, on his sense of utter desolation, and on his realization that he can neither understand nor contest the world of adults.

> His mother devoured him with her eyes and he felt confused. That night, in bed, his eyes opened, he studied the way to straighten out his mistake: he would say only what was absolutely necessary, he would spend more time by himself in the attic; but then, he was carried away by the voices that grew louder and louder, and suddenly, the room was full with a thundering voice and a vocabulary he had never heard before (81).

Richi's feeble consciousness is drowned by the father's words which announce and pronounce into existence an unprecedented world of force and violence. Richi, who will later be known as the Slave, cannot pass from the world of the mother to the law of the father without suffering profound alienation. He is unable to transform his fear and trembling into an act of defiance of the father in order eventually to take his place. Jaguar and Alberto, whose portrait is sketched in the first three segments of the same chapter, seem to be gifted with enough vitality and strength to overcome the negative weight of the father's law and to go on to emulate the adults' macho behavior, with their contempt for the "soft" world of woman, effeminate men, and "slaves."

Vargas Llosa creates a powerful scene for the closing of chapter 3. In the dark, amid the shadows of the night and the disfiguration of a confused consciousness, Richi's memory becomes the stage for the reenactment of a primordial scene of separation from the beloved mother. Such a separation in one way or another divides forever the life of each of the boys in the novel.

> He managed to see his mother's face, deformed under the shaded light of the lamp. He heard her babbling something, but his eyes suddenly perceived a great white silhouette. He thought "he is naked" and he was terrified again. His father hit him with the palm of his hand and he fell down without a sound. But, he immediately got up: everything was swirling around him. . . . From there he could see his mother jumping off the bed. He saw his father turn around and head toward him bellowing. He felt himself hoisted up in the air. . . . Suddenly he was back in his room. It was all dark (82).

The four principal narrators are gathered in chapter 3, as in most of the other chapters, to bring forth an enormous diversity of experience, presented from a multiplicity of angles and modes of perception. There is a certain phenomenological inclination in Vargas Llosa's use of point of view. The narrative, ranging from the neutral third-person semiomniscient narrator to the interior monologue, intends to represent a world of feelings, sensations, emotion, reverie, and action as if the "things" were there by themselves. In that sense Vargas Llosa's narrative craft can be considered an extension of realism's claims to objectivity. This is why Vargas Llosa argues that in his novels the "author" is, like God, absent from his creation. The auctorial voice, the omniscient voice that not only knows the ending of the story but understands its meaning perhaps even better than his characters is never a device or an idea to be found in Vargas Llosa's fictional world. His novelistic world appears unmediated. The illusion of autonomy is accomplished by an extraordinary assembly of the most effective mimetic literary devices.

A further look at Vargas Llosa's craft will show us that part of the reason why his narrative seems so vividly true is because, in the composition of each narrator's point of view, we find further combinations and complexities. Each boy's voice is not simply assigned a certain style or type of point of view. In Alberto's segment in the first chapter we find a combination of different types of enunciations: 1) the exterior, third-person omniscient narrator; 2) an omniscient narrator identified with Alberto; 3) third-person interior monologue; and 4) completely interiorized point of view or stream of consciousness. Their personality and veracity thus emerge with the full complexity and force of a lifelike encounter. Each narrator's voice is marked by different emphases and peculiarities in diction, lexicon, rhythm, and ideology. Consequently point of view is not merely a matter subject to the observers' physical, social, or emotional location in the course of events, but has to do with the individual as a discrete whole, functioning, creating, and responding to his context or historical situation. Each narrator's voice and story are continuously interrupted, and therefore fragmented, by the irrupting presence of a world rendered as change and activity. Fragmentation is thus transformed from a rhetorical device into a world view or even an epistemology. Although character development is minimal and the plot line is very straightforward, the novel itself achieves a perceptible thickness in which nothing remains simple, in which cause and effect appear mediated by a dense layer of contradictions.

Control of Distance: The Masking Tale

Although the world that Vargas Llosa creates seems to present itself in its original primacy to the reader, a very subtle and effective control of distance does in fact govern the implied reader's relation to the life and story of his characters. Distance—affective, intellectual, and idiosyncratic—between the implied reader and the world of the novel is crucial, for it points the way to interpretation. Vargas Llosa as author is never identified with any of the narrators; neither does he show any partiality, nor offer clarification or assistance in interpreting the meaning of their lives or the world in which they struggle to survive. The author appears only by implication, and when he does, he seems removed, equally impartial to the anguish, hopes, and crimes of his creatures. The characters, just like the reader, appear free to make choices and to weave interpretations of acts that, inasmuch as they are human and social, have an inescapable moral or ethical value. In this sense the epigraph taken from Sartre in *The Time of the Hero* seems justified not only by the boys' stories but also by the implied author's stance toward the master story he tells:

> We play the part of heroes because we are cowards, the part of saints because we are wicked; we play at being assassins because we are dying to kill our brothers; we play at being because we are born liars.

Perhaps the best example of the coward in the guise of the valorous knight, the liar in the guise of the honest man, is Alberto. His will to deceive and his skill in self-delusion have been so finely crafted by his experience at home, by the model of his father, by his male peers who "protect" their sisters but see in every other woman a possible prey, that by the time the reader encounters Alberto, he has already been transformed into the Poet. The night of Cava's crime Alberto/the Poet appears to the reader as a sincere young man in need of a miserably small amount of money. The desire for money, in a finely tuned, free-association sequence, is accompanied by the evocation of painful family relations. Fantasy and memory are difficult to untangle in the portrait of Alberto's desire. He imagines himself forgiving his father for the abuse of his mother, provided that the father let him have the money. For the money, Alberto is ready to make the ultimate concession: "As far as I am concerned, you can have all the whores you want, as long as you give me my allowance" (18). The reader emphathizes with Alberto's plight. Twenty *soles,* barely a dollar. There is not much one can buy with a dollar, not even in Peru. Vargas Llosa's technique of holding out on the reader proves to be, once again, crucial in this segment. As Alberto begs and longs for the dollar, we are not told what exactly is the object of his desire. Only the intensity of his desire contrasted with the pitiful amount of money necessary for his happiness appear to be connected. Later we shall find out that the Poet's plan is to spend the dollar at a whorehouse. He would like to have enough money to make love, actually to boast and write about having made love, to the fashionable whore Golden Toes.

The Poet's poignant compassion for his mother's unhappiness and his ready willingness to compromise with his father's cynicism have to be reinterpreted by the reader when the story finally reveals the nature of his desire and the extent of his volition to achieve satisfaction. For "the money" he is not only ready to forgive his father, or rather to cover up for him, but he will also try to profit from the sale of his pornographic little novels: "To make a living out of writing pornographic novels, let them pay me for writing" (18). Alberto/the Poet, the "good," middle-class boy, the boy who commiserates with Richi and helps the Slave steal the shoelaces necessary to avoid punishment, is the same Poet who at the end of the novel will take back all his accusations against The Circle and against Jaguar. In taking it all back, the Poet also recants the whole account of *The Time of the Hero*, for what is the entire story if not the tale of The Circle and Jaguar's murder of the Slave? He, the Poet, has gone beyond the walls of the military academy and sold the reader (you and me) a violent and pornographic story, just as in school he made money indulging the pleasure of his fellow cadets with his little pornographic novels.

The Poet's expertise in lying and pretending to be crazy, keeping his distance from The Circle, amounts to a consummate strategy for survival. As a buffer between the Slave's helplessness and Jaguar's abusive power, between the military hierarchy and the "truth," and between the actual sexual desires of the boys and their sublimated satisfaction in his pornographic writing, the Poet engages a realm of false freedom and false choices. His awareness of the power of his word blends with his money fantasies into a vision of his name in the list of those identified for punishment. At the possibility of his crime and subsequent punishment, the Poet panics; he grows numb in the presence of the lieutenant. As he recovers, the power of the word returns to him, and he decides to fake his way out of his transgression by simulating humility. He tells the lieutenant that he is distressed and wishes to "get some moral advice" from him, although he actually had wanted to lie to the lieutenant and tell him that his father was a general and would punish the officer if he dared punish the son/the Poet. But he decides to tell another lie instead, to invent the anxiety of a false dream: "Sometimes I dream that I kill someone, that animals with human faces chase me. I wake up sweating and trembling. Something awful, Lieutenant, I swear" (20). For the Poet, to speak is to lie, to fantasize, to speak of dreams, and to write novels and accusations of murder. "I want to tell him that my father is a general.... He interrupts himself, for an instant he is uncertain, then he lies" (20).

A finely tuned play of distance and the author's impartiality leave us with an unresolved duality in the boys' character and in the story's denouement. How do we reconcile into one single coherent person and personality the cruel, cynical and callous Jaguar, the probable murderer of Richi, and the tender boy in love with innocent and good Teresa? Because Vargas Llosa gives us the necessary clue only at the very end of the novel, we are forced to review the entire story and take another look at the segments told by the anonymous narrator. But that process of rereading or reconsideration of the novel will also disclose, and even emphasize, the duality and the hypocrisy involved in the making of Alberto, a character assumed by many to be the hero in the story because he had, or had simulated, the courage to denounce the murder and accuse Jaguar of it.

While the Jaguar of the academy remains incompatible with the shy orphan child befriended by Higueras, Alberto's duality emerges as a delicate tissue of cynical deceit and self-delusion. In Alberto/the Poet, as in Richi/Slave, the two selves appear as parts of a single entity cut from the same cloth. This binary formation within the lives of Vargas Llosa's characters will become a stronger and clearer trait in his later novels. The most obvious sign of this duality is the double naming of most of his characters: Alberto/the Poet, Richi/Slave in *The Time of the Hero;* Bonifacia/La Selvática, Lituma/El Sargento, and Anselmo/the Harpist in *The Green House.* This double naming is, of course, not gratuitous; it stands symbolically for the sudden shifts and almost irreconcilable parts, before and after, in social identities and transformations undergone by Vargas Llosa's characters. In this sense Vargas Llosa's characterization is akin to the process of characterization and plot development of the chivalric novel, in which knights as well as the princess often act under an assumed name or a disguised identity. Often the mask of the disguise or the sobriquet given turns out to be the true or rather the lasting identity of the person's character in action. This repeated method of characterization and rationale for and in the plot in turn reveals Vargas Llosa's sense that neither reality nor history can be conceived of as coherent, developmental processes, stretched over a long chronology, itself hinged on a rational series of cause and effect. Individuals and their acts and history appear rather as a splintered conglomeration of data, feeling, perception, and thought so complex as to exceed the bounds of any single model of representation.

NOTE

1. Mario Vargas Llosa, *La ciudad y los perros,* (Barcelona: Seix Barral, 1963) 63. All translations are mine and are from this edition. Page numbers are cited in the text.

CHAPTER THREE

The Green House: Formal Experimentation and Marginal Territories

Published in Barcelona in 1965, *La casa verde* was acclaimed by the critics and devoured by the general readership. Almost immediately after publication it was awarded three important prizes: Spain conferred upon it the Premio de la Crítica (1966); Venezuela awarded it the most important and lucrative international literary prize in Latin America; the Rómulo Gallegos Prize (1967); and Peru, which had publicly burned copies of *The Time of the Hero,* awarded it the Premio Nacional de Novela (1967). Not yet thirty years old, Vargas Llosa found himself a popular, internationally recognized writer. Above all, his work was being accepted and honored by the literary establishment and the state's cultural institutions in Venezuela and Peru. This official recognition did not seem necessarily to square with his stated position as a writer critical of the status quo and supportive of the Cuban revolution. In his acceptance speech, "Literature Is Fire," he took the trouble to remind his elegant audience in Caracas of his intention to remain faithful to his idea of the writer as sentinel and critic of society's abuses and games of deception.

Writing (a year before) to protest the Soviet trials

of the dissident writers Andrey Sinyavsky and Yuri Daniel in "Una insurrección permanente," Vargas Llosa advanced the notion that the writer is essentially an eternally dissatisfied individual:

> No one who lives satisfied is capable of writing dramas, short stories or novels.... No one who agrees with the way things are would attempt the absurdly ambitious enterprise of inventing verbal realities. Politicians, judges, prosecutors and censors, you must understand it once and for all: literature is permanent insurrection.... All attempts to tame its ungovernable nature will fail. Literature may die, but it shall never submit.[1]

In "La literatura es fuego" he pursued the same argument and almost repeated some of the words, phrases and ideas used to defend the writer's freedom in the essay on the two Soviet dissident writers. He confronted his Latin American audience with its traditional suspicious, shabby, and even vindictive attitude towards its writers:

> Without editorial publishing houses, without readers, without a cultural atmosphere that could encourage and give incentive to him, the Latin American writer has been a man who fought battles knowing from the beginning that he was already a defeated man. His choice of vocation was not accepted by society, it was merely tolerated.[2]

The author of *The Green House* warned his audience that while he was appearing before them to receive the Rómulo Gallegos Prize, a prize created by the Venezuelan government to honor the author of *Doña Bárbara* (1929) and former president of the country, he had no intention of being coopted. While he acknowledged that conditions for the Latin American writer had begun to improve with the remarkable growth of the reading public and a generally friendlier atmosphere toward writers, it was, nevertheless, necessary to recognize the possibility of a new danger:

> The same societies that rejected and exiled the writer can now think that it is more efficient and convenient to assimilate the writer, to extend him a sort of official position. That is why it is necessary to remind our societies of what is in store for them. It is necessary to caution them, and remind them, that literature is fire. That means dissidence and rebellion; for the raison d'être of the writer is to protest, to contradict, and to criticize.[3]

Public speeches such as "La literatura es fuego" and journalistic essays on the Cuban revolution and the writer's commitment to freedom and dissent, earned for Vargas Llosa a special place in news-making interviews. In one such interview with the Mexican writer and journalist Elena Poniatowska, Vargas Llosa discusses not only his literary passions but also the making of *The Green House*.[4] He carefully traces his literary voyage from the enclosure of the military academy to the vast expanses of Peru's jungles and deserts, from the old colonial centers of Peruvian life to its contemporary marginal territories. Poniatowska seems unusually impressed with the passion and commitment of a writer who openly speaks of the suffering he endured while writing his new novel. In the preface to *Antología mínima* the author of *Hasta no verte Jesús mío* (1969) and *La Noche de Tlatelolco* (1968) assures her reader that in the case of this young novelist "one is completely convinced that for this writer, writing is his whole life, if he could not write he would kill himself. . . . Next to him Alejo Carpentier is a mere academic."

In this interview with Poniatowska, Vargas Llosa also recalls that when he was in fifth grade, living in Piura,

> one of the myths that circulated among us schoolboys was the story of the whorehouse on the outskirts of town, right in the middle of the desert, across the river. It was a rustic wooden house. All painted in green! . . . We called it "the green house." . . . Five years later I returned to Piura, I was then a high school senior, the green house was still there and its attraction had not vanished. At that time I already frequented whorehouses and so I discovered what "the green house" was like inside.[5]

His discovery of the jungle took place a few years later on a trip organized by Peruvian anthropologists to the Upper Marañón. Vargas Llosa recalls that his voyage to the jungle meant for him an emotional upheaval as great perhaps as his experience in the military academy. Peru appeared an even vaster and more frightening reality than the Leoncio Prado Academy. He was totally confused by the "civilizing" enterprise of the Spanish nuns, which he likens to a factory without materials for processing. Without possible souls for evangelizing, the nuns decided that their mission was to steal the Aguaruna girls from their parents and culture, take them to their school, and "civilize" them there.

Vargas Llosa also recounts for Poniatowska how he came upon the story of Fushía, perhaps the mother lode for *The Green House*. In the same trip to the Upper Marañón he was introduced to a young Aguaruna girl who had fled the harem of a Japanese warlord: "She did not speak Spanish. Through an interpreter, she told me her story and the story of the Japanese Fushía. That man had lived on his island for thirty years, in complete disregard of the law, very much like a feudal lord or one of those Italian condottieri."[6]

How to weave all these diverse and tormenting stories into a unified novel was to become a major problem for Vargas Llosa. Not only did events take place in very different societies and settings, but the jungle as a scenario of life and representation had a long tradition in both Latin American and European letters. Vargas Llosa was, of course, conscious of masterpieces such as Kipling's *The Jungle Book* (1894), Horacio Quiroga's *Historias de amor, de locura y de muerte* [Stories of love, madness, and death], and what he considered failed *indigenista* novels such as *La vorágine* (1924 [*The Vortex,* 1935]) by José Eustasio Rivera, or *Los pasos perdidos* (1953 [*The Lost Steps,* 1956]) by Alejo Carpentier, novels in which, for him, nature became the protagonist, thus killing the story.

When he first began writing his second novel, he intended to write about "the green house" only. But he found that Fushía, Bonifacia, Jum, and Santa María de Nieva kept breaking into the text about Piura and the bohemian foursome of the *Inconquistables*. In desperation he decided to write two novels at the same time: "I thought that writing two novels would cause me less anxiety than writing just one. I thought that going back and forth, from one novel to the other, would prove refreshing, rejuvenating. It was a grave mistake. It turned out to be the opposite."[7]

As time went on, the project proved impossible. Every day he faced a growing sense of confusion. Keeping the characters and settings apart demanded enormous concentration. In the end he gave up the struggle to keep Santa María de Nieva apart from Piura, Bonifacia away from the green house, and Lituma stationed in Piura. He decided to allow the inner workings of his imagination to dictate the shape and structure of the new world of the novel.

In choosing the details for the musicians of the green house, Vargas Llosa's recollection of Piura proved insufficient. His earlier reading of Dumas came, once again, to enrich and round out the spectrum of novelistic possibilities. Bola's imposing physique thus blended or contrasted with a kind heart, in the style of Porthos in *The Three Musketeers* and Lotario in *Mandrake, the Magician*. Recalling the making of Anselmo, Vargas Llosa writes:

> In Anselmo I resuscitated a character dear to all enthusiasts of the chivalric novel and Western adventures: the foreigner who arrives in a strange city and takes it over. I have always had a weak spot for the melodramatic Mexican film. So, in order to "humanize" the stranger, I added to Anselmo's story a sentimental truculent episode. For that, I used my recollection of a novel by Paul Bowles, *El ciego protector*.[8]

Instead of creating a blind Anselmo, as in Bowles's novel, Vargas Llosa visits the blindness on the girl whom the Peruvian harpist seduces. This truculent detail, Vargas Llosa admits, made it very difficult for him to imagine and render the love scenes between Anselmo and Antonia, because he felt that the girl's blindness and innocence stretched the limits of the credible. He resolved this problem, he says, by infusing the voice of the narrator of the story with a very strong sense of ambiguity.

If rendering Anselmo's repeated seductions of Antonia stretched the limits of verisimilitude, Vargas Llosa had yet another formidable problem of credibility to resolve: how to portray a jungle with which he was unfamiliar. He tried to overcome his ignorance of tropical fauna and flora by reading everything he could find in the Paris libraries. In *Historia secreta de una novela,* Vargas Llosa writes that for a whole year he read nothing but books on the Amazon Basin, from seventeenth-century chronicles, including Antonio Rodríguez de León Pinelo's *El Paraíso en el Nuevo Mundo,* to the many "Amazonian novels" written by other Latin American authors. He found the last group especially objectionable, because he feels that these novels are dominated by a "demagogic fauna and flora, a descriptive frenzy and great truculence."[9]

In view of this assessment he decided to abandon any attempt to describe the jungle. *The Green House,* like all his narratives, brings in only snippets of descriptive matter. In fact, setting is generally derived from the fragmented perception of the narrator's surroundings. There are never block descriptions of rooms, gardens, garments, or landscapes in the novels of Vargas Llosa. Having come to grips with some of the major obstacles in the coalescence of these two (Santa Maria de Nieva and Piura) militantly separate worlds, Vargas Llosa found that his novel could actually come alive if he remained faithful to the chief characteristic of his novelistic craft and world: emphasis on action. Just as in Dumas, the chivalric novel, and Westerns, in *The Green House* we find a world caught in entropic action that gives place to more exciting action, often at the expense of coherence and meaning. It seems that the most appropriate means to render such action into narrative form is, once again, the fragment. *The Green House* posits the fragment as its key epistemological unit and, by doing so, represents the world as a continuous and unstable rotation of signs.

The Plot

The Green House possesses no dominant story line under which the lateral lines can be subsumed. Depending on the empathies of the reader, some have argued that Anselmo's story, Fushía's story, or Bonifacia's story constitutes the major plot. The narrative of the novel covers three stories which at times intersect, since some of the characters in any given plot also play a small part in another. Lituma, Bonifacia, and Lalita become the points of intersection for the stories that take place in the jungle (the stories of Jum, the nuns, Reátegui, Aquilino, and Fushía) as well as for the stories set in Piura (the stories of Anselmo, Antonia, Chunga, the Champs, Father García, and Juana Baura). As a whole, the novel covers the lives of three generations and a total of thirty-four characters.

The multiplicity of the novel's segments, as well as the variety of the adventures that compose each story, can actually be regarded as three main axes: Lituma-Bonifacia; Aquilino-Lalita; and Anselmo-Antonia. This pairing corresponds to an amorous criterion, and as in most love stories the pair soon dissolves into a triangle.

The Lituma-Bonifacia pair translates into three different triangles, depending on Bonifacia's location. In Santa María de Nieva the triangle includes Lalita, who acts as the go-between for the Sergeant's marriage to the runaway from the nuns' convent. In Piura the pair Bonifacia-Lituma is intervened by the Champs, Lituma's friends whose idea it is to rape Bonifacia, rename her La Selvática, and have her work as a prostitute in the green house. The same Lituma-Bonifacia pair is later intervened by La Chunga, who establishes La Selvática's rights to her own wages.

Fushía's main erotic attachment is to Lalita, who in the course of events not only is his main sexual partner but also bears him a son. This pair is turned into a triangle by the fact that Lalita had been, before Fushía, Reátegui's adolescent concubine. Later she leaves Fushía to become Nieves's common-law wife. The pair Fushía-Lalita is further triangulated by the shared, fatherlike image they each have in Aquilino.

Juana Baura, Antonia's adoptive mother, constitutes at first the third point in the relationship between Anselmo and Toñita. This oppositional function is later taken up by Father García, who like Juana Baura opposes with all his might Anselmo's union with the young girl and his house of prostitution. Furthermore, the novel's vast retrospective centers on a pair of institutions—the army and the church—as the pivots around which both the gathering and pairing of characters is arranged. This pair also dissolves into a triangle. The third point of tension and balance or imbalance is, of course, civilian society and its own two main centers for encounter and dispersion: marriage and prostitution.

The novel begins with a scene of kidnapping and theft. Two nuns, dressed inappropriately in heavy, long robes, glide down a jungle river in a navy boat. They are assisted and protected by a number of soldiers. Their mission is to bargain for or abduct as many girls as they can find in the camps of the Aguaruna people. In a bewildering and convulsing opening segment marked by an inescapable feeling of immediacy, the reader witnesses the capture of several girls. Later, the reader's memory will provide the necessary links in the realization that Bonifacia was one of the girls captured that afternoon. Hiding the identity of the girl here is one of Vargas Llosa's favorite techniques that works to heighten the enigmatic quality of his plots. Depriving the reader of key informational elements at the "appropriate" juncture displaces the moment of denouement and equivocates the significance of acts and events in the plot. But most especially this technique of denial of information, which Vargas Llosa calls the Hemingway technique of the missing elements, causes the reader to reevaluate the sequences operating in the plot, and the meaning or meanings of the story when all the relevant data are finally available. The harm and hurt done to Bonifacia will seem even greater and less forgivable when we eventually realize that the kidnapped girl is not only

Jum's daughter but the very same Selvática working as a prostitute in the green house to support the good times that the Champs regard as their birthright.

Briefly, the Aguaruna girl is kidnapped by the nuns and soldiers. She is taken prisoner to the nuns' school where, along with other girls kidnapped during previous expeditions, she is to be "civilized." When the girls have grown up, the nuns must make room for new recruits. The girls, or rather the young women, are placed as servants in the homes of army officers. Bonifacia, a distinguished and trusted pupil, stays a bit longer at the convent, helping the nuns deal with the bellicose, "selvatic," or rather resisting manners of the fresh recruits. In a seemingly arbitrary act, she decides to let a new group of pathetic and frightened little girls escape. For this breach of trust she is expelled from the convent and thrown onto the streets of Santa María de Nieva. There she meets Lalita, who at the time lives in the same jungle frontier town.

Bonifacia enters Lalita's home as a servant. Nieves has a friend known as the Sergeant, and Lalita suggests that Bonifacia would make a good wife for him. It would seem that Bonifacia, the story's heroine, has managed to escape a terrible destiny of rape and servitude. But Bonifacia's story is at this point far from over. The Sergeant is transferred back to his native Piura. There, his name is simply Lituma, one of the Champs from the Mangachería, a place on the outskirts of the city where criminals and drunkards live, proud of their ungovernable traditions. In Piura the Champs contemptuously rename Bonifacia La Selvática.

In a senseless game of something like Russian roulette Lituma kills a prominent local landowner. He is sentenced to ten years in jail in Lima, and he entrusts his wife to his friends. During his absence they get her drunk and rape her. Ashamed, Bonifacia/La Selvática aborts. Penniless and friendless, she accepts work in the green house. When Lituma comes back, he is devastated to find Bonifacia/La Selvática at the green house. A true macho, he is however more resentful of her "betrayal" than of his male friend's betrayal. Lituma/the Sergeant soon settles down to live on Bonifacia/La Selvática's income.

In the general chronology of the time of the novel Bonifacia's story takes place in the immediate past. The stories of Jum and Fushía fit into a middle segment, and Anselmo's is probably the story set into the past furthest removed from the present. When Bonifacia goes to work at the green house, the proprietor of the establishment is La Chunga, the tough daughter of Toñita and Anselmo, now an old blind harpist.

Anselmo, not unlike the rest of the characters in the novel, seems to emerge out of nowhere. As with Bonifacia, Fushía, Lalita, Nieves, Aquilino, and Lituma, his whole being is encapsulated in a single name. Last names are infrequent in *The Green House,* since genealogy as an anchor to history, to a shared and meaningful past, is absent in this novel. The same emphasis on the present is true for the rest of Vargas Llosa's fictional world. While Anselmo is not re-named upon his arrival in Piura, his individuality is marked by a simple allusion to his trade. Within the social and economic structure of a town like Piura it suffices for him to be known as Anselmo the harpist. While identification by first name only would be enough for a man living at the fringes of society and the law, his total absence of origins seems nevertheless atypical in a stable, traditional, and colonial society. In towns such as Piura or the Mangachería, even very poor and illiterate people know a great deal about their ancestry and family origins. Anselmo literally emerges out of the desert. The man without a past becomes a formidable challenge to Piura's fossilized values and imagination.

Anselmo's story appears inextricable from Toñita's, even before the stranger befriends and kidnaps the adolescent girl from one of Piura's parks. Toñita's origins appear lost in the desert too. Like Anselmo's, her story is pieced together from the generalized recollection of Piura's gossip. The town's own version maintains that Toñita is the daughter of a well-to-do couple who in a trip across the desert were set upon by a band of legendary bandits. It seems that the adults were all robbed and killed, and that the little girl was also left for dead. The vultures devoured the human carcasses. In the case of the little girl they had already begun to pluck her eyes out when another group of travelers found her. Miraculously, she did not die. The dry heat of the desert healed the wounds of her eye sockets, but it also left her deaf and mute.

Juana Baura, a washerwoman, takes in the little girl and raises her as her own. She takes Toñita everywhere with her. The little girl has a lovely face and in a few years grows into a beautiful pubescent girl. Often, to avoid taking the girl to all her delivery and pick-up stops, Juana leaves Toñita sitting on a park bench. There Anselmo sees her for the first time and falls for her, infatuated by her silent beauty. He kidnaps Toñita, rapes her, and takes her to live with him in the tower of the green house, where he plays the harp. Later, Toñita dies while giving birth to a baby girl, La Chunga. Soon afterward, a large group of incensed women led by the scandalized and firebrand Father García burn down the green house. Years later, the second house rises in the desert like a phoenix. It is owned by La Chunga. Anselmo, an old man now, plays the harp.

Several critics, among them Dick Gerdes, feel that Anselmo's desire for Toñita "undergoes a lyrical metamorphosis in the novel. Like the Brothel itself, their love is a source of subjectivity, deep-seated, titillating, unsatisfied fantasy of unrepented lust. It is also a fountainhead of passion and tenderness that arouses pity and even causes Anselmo (and the reader) to feel human again."[10]

Other readers, unable to forget how Anselmo arbitrarily separated Toñita from her devoted adoptive mother, and how all the erotic desire and the consciousness of feeling is portrayed from Anselmo's point of view exclusively, find it difficult to empathize with the so-called lyricism of the scenes in which Anselmo makes "love" to the blind-deaf-mute girl. As I see it, the irony of this whole episode is that Anselmo, like the nuns, rationalizes his desire as yet another civilizing enterprise. He thinks he can bring new freedom to the old-fashioned, sexually inhibited people of Piura. Anselmo's funeral takes place some fifty years after he appeared in the town's plaza. Old and decrepit, Father García conducts the funeral rites for the man once hated and condemned to hell.

With Fushía's story Vargas Llosa peripherally touches on the last stages of the ravaging rubber boom of the Amazon Basin. This is the same historical period that the Colombian novel *La vorágine* (1924 [*The Vortex,* 1935]) and the Brazilian saga *Terras do sem fim* (1943 [*The Violent Land,* 1945]) had masterfully fictionalized. In *The Green House* a defeated, lonely, and very ill Fushía tells his own story. Fleeing the police, Fushía and his old friend Aquilino journey downriver by night. Their destination is the San Pablo leper colony. Referring to the ending of his novel, Vargas Llosa says that he felt great pathos for this man. In fact, when he wrote the last lines in which Fushía reluctantly and pathetically begs Aquilino to come back to visit him, the author shed tears for his character's utter loneliness.

Sometime in the 1920s Fushía had escaped jail and fled his native Brazil. Penniless but ambitious, he set out to look for work in Iquitos, Peru. In his version of his life adventures Fushía will claim innocence of the original crime for which he was jailed. In Iquitos he meets Julio Reátegui, a crooked businessman and affluent landowner. Fushía runs Reátegui's hotel accounts. From his master he learns all the tricks of legal theft. Discovered by Reátegui, and having bought the pubescent Lalita from her own mother, he flees once more into the depths of the Peruvian jungle. Fushía's obsession is to become a wealthy man. On the Santiago River, near the border with Ecuador, Fushía settles on a virtually inaccessible island. There, with the help of the warriors of the Huambisa people, he sets himself up as a warlord. In search of rubber and women, he raids the nearby Amazonian native communities. Fushía reigns over his territory, possessions, and army as a true autocrat. The monomaniacal, frantic little man of Japanese descent lives in constant fear of being found out by Reátegui. He sells his rubber to the same contraband dealers who bought rubber from Reátegui and who in turn sell it to suppliers of rubber for the Axis powers. The European war seems distant indeed from the Amazon Basin, but the horrors visited upon the inhabitants of capitalism's frontier are comparable only to the Holocaust in Europe during the Second World War.

During the twenty-five-year span encompassed by the novel's action in the Amazon Basin, the culture of the native people of the area is ruthlessly destroyed by the penetration of national and international economic and cultural forces. Bonifacia's life is one example of penetration and destruction at the cultural level. Although Jum's destruction is brought on more directly by economic forces, the general contempt which Peruvians and foreigners hold for Indians allows for the terror and isolation affecting Jum. The story of this man, though secondary, is intimately connected to Fushía's thirst for wealth, Reátegui's political hold on the region, and Bonifacia's eventual prostitution. Jum, an Aguaruna chief, aware of the money that the rubber trade brings in for Reátegui and others, and aided by the local schoolteachers, decides to create a producers' cooperative that will bypass middlemen like Fushía. For rebelling against the rubber trade monopoly and under orders from Reátegui (the governor of Santa María de Nieva) Jum is hanged upside down and tortured. What is worse, he is culturally emasculated when his hair is cut off. As a consequence of this symbolic act of regicide he loses his position as tribal leader. He is left to roam the world, forever cut from his roots, his community, and his purpose in life. As with Fushía's story, the destruction of Jum is based on the life a person Vargas Llosa met in his first trip to the Peruvian jungle.

In war and in sex Fushía is perpetual motion; the satisfaction of his desire for wealth, women, and power seems impossible. A harem of native women is not enough, because Fushía "aspires" to the satisfaction of his sexual appetites with white women. This is why Lalita is his principal concubine. Being the supreme warlord in the territory of the Santiago River is also less than satisfactory. Fushía's desire is to rival Reátegui within the "civilized" territories of Iquitos or Santa María de Nieva. His hopes and desires are wrecked when the undeniable evidence of leprosy begins to affect his feet and legs. In retrospect, Lalita tells Aquilino that she first suspected Fushía's illness when he began refusing to take his boots off even to make love or rest in his hammock. Later, when the stench of his feet becomes unbearable and his tantrums become more frequent and even more abusive, she decides to take her son, flee the island, and abandon Fushía to his Huambisa allies and concubines.

As the lives of the chief characters ebb and reach a final resting point in either death or supreme degradation, the plots of the novel come to a halt. The multiple structure of the narrative and the symmetrical arrangement of the division of narrative elements make it difficult for the reader to establish any reasonable or typical explanation with regard to why things happen the way they do. Each character, summed up in the totality of events and experiences of his or her life, seems a mere asteroid traveling a capricious route through an exploding universe. The sense of alienation felt by each character and encapsulated in the formal elements of the narrative becomes the hallmark of *The Green House*.

Structure, Organization, and Meaning

The organizational technique of *The Green House*, as well as its world view, is fragmented, complex, mobile, and alienating. From the very beginning of the book the reader is bewildered, fascinated, manipulated, estranged, and overwhelmed. Yet the novel conforms to a strict organizational pattern that controls effectively the infusion of informational material, the multiplicity of points of view, and the distance between the sites of enunciation (narrators) and the reader's intellectual and affective world. If the novel actually were the chaos that it first appears to be, it would not be as masterfully efficient in creating the truth of its fiction, nor could it sustain the reader's fascinated gaze upon the canvas that it develops over its intense 400 pages. What Vargas Llosa offers in *The Green House*, as in the rest of his novels, is a carefully crafted instrument of knowledge which allows him and his reader the privileged moment of gazing upon an ever-changing historical reality.

Unlike the European nineteenth-century novelist or the regionalist Latin American writer, Vargas Llosa cannot afford to create the illusion that the external world of perception—houses, landscapes, woods, gardens, clothing fashions, manner of speech, occupations, social and economic class, nations, regions, religious beliefs, manners—is in any way a stable entity. Stability of the external world gives way in Vargas Llosa's world to a phenomenological flux. This emphasis on the instability of the world gives his novels their modern flavor. However, it is compensated for by a static modulation in the portrayal of the inner being of his characters. Fushía, Bonifacia, Anselmo, Alberto, and Jaguar do not transcend the stereotypical dimension. Their circumstances may change drastically, just as their names do, but the inner workings of the person remain the same. While the plots grow and move ahead through the novel, while the sheer number of adventures thickens the world of the narrative, the characters do not develop. Original traits are not modified by experience so that the envious man may learn to be generous, the trusting, naïve girl to be cautious and wary, and the ferocious little man to modulate the intensity and foolishness of his desire. A comparison with Dickens's and Trollope's treatment of character and plot shows how far Vargas Llosa's world view stands from those of the nineteenth-century English masters of the realistic novel. The ever good, ever healthy, ever energetic hero of the chivalric novel and the Western, the one-dimensional bad guy Reátegui, or the gigantic but good-hearted Porthos constitute the agents of the plot of adventures (action in the world) of Vargas Llosa's fictional universe.

Simple time and space relationships appear broken in the tales of the characters' adventures. Discontinuity in the events which together make up what we call a life is unmistakably marked by the discontinuity in the characters' names or nicknames. Dick Gerdes writes that "the discontinuous nature of the events produces the illusion of simultaneity. As a consequence, human events are relegated to a repetitious, cyclical and almost timeless flow of isolated, senseless, present moments. The process effaces human individuality."[11]

Not only time and space are discarded as the chief "natural" elements for organizational continuity. Causality is another traditional element of developmental illusion that Vargas Llosa sacrifices in his search for the primacy of the present. Specific actions, feelings, thoughts, fantasies, and even periods in characters' experiences remain isolated. Each fragment, like a film's take, stands out in its sheer and powerful intensity. The sense of immediacy conveyed to the reader is thus heightened to a maximum point of "realism." And yet all the fragments, like an Inca wall, hold together, forever bonded by an invisible glue. The secret is once again to be found in the subconscious thematic dovetailing and the rigorous arrangement of the main rhetorical elements.

The novel is divided into several major blocks. Each of these large parts is in turn subdivided into smaller units, and each of these smaller units is in turn dedicated to the reconstruction of a major event in the life of a character. It is this last purpose that calls for all the techniques of multiplicity of narrators, chaotic mixing of times, spaces, voices, and chronologies. It is at the level of reconstruction where the often noted and praised dialogues take over the narrative flow, and where all possible juxtapositions come to fruition.

The narrative of *The Green House* is divided into four large sections and an epilogue. Sections 1 and 3, as well as the Epilogue, each have four chapters. Sections 2 and 4 contain three chapters each. By itself, this alternation marks a syncopated rhythm. At the same time it builds a sense of symmetry in the flow of the reading experience. The beginning of each chapter constitutes a sort of portico to each part. This overture is generally organized by the consciousness of an omniscient narrator capable of orchestrating the multiple points of view of several participant characters. It sets the tone, quality, and thematic undercurrents for the section that it introduces. As in *The Time of the Hero,* each of the four or three chapters of each section is in turn divided into segments. The Epilogue, however, is all a single unit. It has no chapters or segments, though in retrospect the portico's chief function is to provide information needed for later clarification of linear sequences of events. The Epilogue's long duration flows in a graphic continuum eschewed in the main body of the novel. The Epilogue's unbroken flow would appear to privilege its recapitulating position. It is clearly marked as closure.

The general pattern of the novel's arrangement of materials relies on the principle of variation within repetition, alternation of similar elements, combination of variable factors, constant mobility, and displacement of comparable ingredients. The opening of the novel—the scene in which the nuns and soldiers kidnap the Aguaruna girls—is an excellent example, a kind of aleph of Vargas Llosa's dazzling narrative resources.

"The Sergeant takes a look at Sister Patrocinio and the botfly is still there."[12] This single sentence exemplifies Vargas Llosa's use of present tense to portray events which by definition are past events, for fictional and historical actions belong in the past. The same sentence also illustrates Vargas Llosa's mastery of speed and economy that produce in the reader's consciousness the sense of unmediated presence before the reality represented on the printed page. In this sentence the reader, as privileged observer, seems to be physically standing just behind the Sergeant. The reader sees the Sergeant taking a look at Sister Patrocinio, who is not only within the Sergeant's visual scope but, by implication, also within the reader's own visual field. "And the botfly is still there" creates, on the one hand, a retrospective consciousness of the event in the reader's mind, because "still there" implies that both the reader and the Sergeant had taken a previous look at the nun's face and had then seen the botfly, which was still there. "The botfly is still there" represents, on the other hand, someone's evaluation of the botfly and the space in which it rests. That someone, the reader is led to assume, must be the same Sergeant who "takes a look." Since we are not told that the Sergeant *said* that the botfly was still there, we must assume that the assessment on the permanence of the botfly on its earlier position is a thought occurring in the Sergeant's consciousness or, perhaps, the consciousness of an omniscient narrator whose position coincides with the location of the reader. At this point the reader is firmly set in the position of enjoying a double, unmediated observational post. He or she can shift speedily from the Sergeant's gaze, follow it to the nun's features, focus on the botfly, and also burrow into the Sergeant's consciousness, all in the speed of a short sentence.

In his dexterity with compression Vargas Llosa avoids the "heaviness" of description. This sentence plunges the reader into a world made familiar by the swiftness with which the information is related and by the immediacy of the temporal and spatial frames in which it is contained. If we imagine a movie director organizing the narrative, what we have in that scene is a close-up. Rather than a long and prolonged aerial shot of the jungle, or a depthless view of the river gorge emphasizing the nature of the background for the events, what we have in the opening sentence of *The Green House* is a close-up of the action. The entire portico—a single, eleven-page paragraph—will continue to focus on the action. The background will be foregrounded, but strictly as that upon which the action takes place. This is why Vargas Llosa in the end decided not to describe the immensity of the jungle, for the jungle per se is for him an incidental setting for the monumental drama that the desire and action of his characters develop. Many a reader of course will feel that the jungle setting is a determining part of the novel's entire character.

Avoiding prefatory information on the past of the characters or the reasons why a sergeant and a nun—Humphrey Bogart and Katharine Hepburn in *The African Queen*—find themselves within each other's visual field, the second sentence of the novel, still holding on to the present, states: "The boat is pitching on the muddy waters, between the walls of trees that exhale a burning, sticky breath." In one sentence the location, and above all the "familiar" sensory value of the hot, steamy, endlessly boring Amazonian forest, have been established for a reader who, like the men and the Sergeant, can only react to the jungle's environment with the values of an outsider. The anthropological relation of culture to natural resources, or the astonished and estranged phantasmagoric description of a narrative like *The Lost Steps,* or of movies like Werner Herzog's *Fitzcarraldo,* has no place in *The Green House,* for the consciousness of the jungle in this novel is limited to the consciousness of plain folks (outsiders) trapped in the act of survival at any cost. People like Bonifacia and Fushía are not interested in erecting a whole epistemology based on their observations of the jungle's ecosystem. For them nature is the jungle *is* nature and not a baroque system or a series of pornographic acts, as it appears to Carpentier and Herzog respectively.

Shorty, Fats, Sister Angélica, Sister Patrocinio, Blondy, and the Sergeant do not constitute a scientific, aesthetic, or anthropological expedition. To the contrary, and much to their discomfort, they see their time in the jungle in terms of a boring assignment for which they did not volunteer. The jungle emerges in *The Green House* within the confines of the characters' values, feelings, desires, and cultural parameters. This is why the portico, like the rest of the novel, incorporates on a wholesale basis the voices of the characters into the constitution of the novel's world. The first sentence embodies the Sergeant's point of view. Although the second sentence could be attributed to a nonparticipant semiomniscient narrator, the tense and the immediate reference to the other people in the boat by their nickname only indicate an insider's appreciation and deployment of observation, sensation, and interpretation of the situation on the boat which must also be attributed to the Sergeant. Blondy's streamy sweating, Blacky's grunts, the circling wasps and botflies, and the snoring and choking of the motor are bodily sensory events that can be perceived and registered only by a consciousness focused upon them in close-up fashion.

As closure to the frame in which the body's functions are posited as the seat of perception, a sentence appears that demands attribution to an individualized speaker: "Those jungle people were not normal, why didn't they sweat like the rest of us Christians?" (9). While this rhetorical, unattributable question closes the frame on sweating and its differential meaning, it introduces the jungle peoples and, even more significantly, it brings up the fact that *they* are different from "us," that is, from the soldiers, the nuns, and "us" the readers who by definition have been enveloped within the point of view of "us" Christians. The jungle peoples do not sweat. The notion of "us Christians" extends a bridge to the next close-up. This time the focus is on Sister Angélica. Previous writing conventions would have probably dictated that a new paragraph could begin there. But the relentless speed and cinematic progression of the "takes" and frames in *The Green House* forbid and preclude breaks. Graphic and ocular continuity and contiguity constitute an attempt to overpower the logical fragmentation of the narrative materials.

The enunciation, focusing on Sister Angélica, would seem to arise from the consciousness of an omniscient narrator: "Sitting stiffly in the stern, Sister Angélica keeps her eyes closed, her face is criss-crossed by at least a thousand wrinkles, at times she sticks out the very tip of her tongue, sips up the sweat of her moustache and spits" (9). The vocabulary here seems to belong to the same type of enunciation that described the soldiers' half-naked bodies. There is a certain distance in the tone and a descriptive precision that differentiates this enunciation from the emotional value embodied in the next sentence: "Poor old woman, she wasn't up to these chores." The unmediated juxtaposition of the two types of enunciation, tone, distance, point of view, and emotional charge amount to a dialogic relation between a somewhat emotionally distant observer and a vitally engaged commentator. As in a pointillistic canvas, one color is spattered over another, and yet a third and fourth and fifth color is in turn spattered over the basic mix, so that the different points eventually establish a new kind of *trompe l'oeil*. This *trompe l'oeil* is not one of depth, as in realism, but rather the illusion of continuity in simultaneity.

In the portico of *The Green House,* Vargas Llosa makes maximum use of the technique called assimilated dialogue. Dialogue is not set out on the printed page as separate and discrete discourse. It is not framed as a snatch of reality taken by the omniscient narrator and reproduced on the page in its own immanence. On the contrary, characters' speeches in *The Green House* are incorporated, without any quotation marks, into the main flow of the narrative. While on the boat the Sergeant, Nieves, and the nuns exchange opinions about how they should proceed now that they are approaching the Aguarunas' river landing. Vargas Llosa converts this dialogue exchange into part of the action by eliminating the reporting frame of "said . . . " followed by what was said, in quotation marks. Sometimes enough information is provided so that the reader may discern who said what, but the quotation often flows by without clear attribution, as we saw in the case of "poor old woman, she wasn't up to these chores."

Immediately after the comment on old Sister Angélica the narrative returns to the circling botfly and, without any warning, tells

> and the pilot goes to turn off the motor, they were getting there, Sergeant, Chicais was beyond the gorge. But the Sergeant knew in his heart that there wouldn't be anybody there (9).

If we reset these two sentences in traditional typography and rhetoric, an operation which our mind carries out, in the first reading at least, what we witness is a surprising reversal of tenses and a redistribution of the materials under the exigencies of attribution. The rewritten paragraph would read thus:

> The pilot thought that they were arriving at their destination. He decided to turn off the motor. But before doing so, he alerted the Sergeant and said: "We are getting there, Sergeant. Chicais is just beyond the gorge."
>
> But the Sergeant knew in his heart that there wouldn't be anybody there.

In the comparison between the two narrative rhetorics, it is easy to see how Vargas Llosa's omissions in his use of assimilated dialogue economizes and speeds up his storytelling.

Furthermore, omission in *The Green House,* more so than in *The Time of the Hero,* causes the constant and intense use of shift in point of view. On the first page of the novel the point of view shifts a total of eight times. The first words of the novel plunge the reader into the world of the Sergeant: 1) "The Sergeant takes a look." After this first sentence the semiomniscient narrator takes over: 2) “The boat is pitching.” After the scene about the snorts and sweaty bodies we hear this from Nieves: 3) “These jungle peoples . . .” Then the narrator takes over again with a portrait of Sister Angélica: 4) “Stiff by the stern . . .” At this point, either the Sergeant or Nieves assesses the sister’s situation: 5) “Poor old woman . . .” Another shift takes us from the thought about the old woman in the boat on a jungle river to the practical matter of shutting off the motor of the boat. Nieves’s speech breaks into the portrait of the sister: 6) “They were getting there, Sergeant.” The Sergeant’s hunch follows: 7) “There wouldn’t be anyone there.” Then the narrator provides a closure: 8) “The sound of the engine stops.”

While we have seen how point of view, assimilated dialogue, and omission work at the level of texture (the palpable but not always conscious level of reading or writing), many of Vargas Llosa’s most dazzling narrative strategies belong in the larger, structural level of deployment.

Students of Vargas Llosa’s work have written extensively on his narrative technique. Many of his innovations have been described by different names. Nevertheless, critics such as José Miguel Oviedo, Dick Gerdes, Julio Ortega, and Jean Franco agree on the general dualistic, disjunctive, and interpolated nature of his narrative art. Montage and juxtaposition are probably the most encompassing terms used to convey an idea and feeling about the novel’s architecture. Some have described his telescoped dialogues, that is, setting one conversation within the framing of another ongoing conversation. I have written about the montage and the dual spiral pattern of juxtaposition of scenes set in reverse order of causality. Other critics have taken Vargas Llosa's own terminology for the description of his narrative technique and have written about sets of "Chinese boxes," "communicating vessels," and juxtaposition of "objective and subjective levels of reality."

One of the most systematic and thorough analyses of technique in *The Green House* is Luis A. Diez's *Mario Vargas Llosa's Pursuit of the Total Novel.* In that book Diez shows how closely allied are Vargas Llosa's description of the narrative technique he observes and admires in Joanot Martorell's *Tirant lo Blanc* and his own practices in *The Green House.* Making extensive and careful use of Vargas Llosa's prefatory essay to the 1968 edition of *Tirant lo Blanc,* Diez demonstrates that Vargas Llosa's and Martorell's narrative strategies—"communicating vessels," "temporal distortions," "qualitative jumps," "Chinese boxes," and "different planes of reality"—can be found in full dynamics in *The Green House.* Vargas Llosa envisions his "communicating vessels" technique as a system in which the qualities of one element circulate, like a liquid, around and through another element to produce eventually the "qualitative jump." As an illustration of this technique Vargas Llosa makes reference to the erotic episode in *Tirant lo Blanc,* "Las bodas sordas y el sueño de Placerdemivida." In this scene the promised but undelivered love scene between Princess Carmesina and Tirant is suddenly interrupted in its present sequence by a frame from the future. Vargas Llosa reasons that this temporal distortion is created in order to leave a certain ambiguity and also to maintain reader expectation and curíosity about what actually happened in Carmesina's bedroom. Next day, the narrative takes up the scene but what was then present is now past, and the amorous play is revealed in and as Placerdemivida's dream.[13]

This procedure of cutting the present flow of events by injecting action taking place in the future, which in turn eventually returns full circle to a point in the past or the origin of the action, is repeatedly used in *The Green House*. Diez shows, for instance, how the Anselmo-Toñita love story follows a pattern similar to the Carmesina-Tirant episode. A breakdown of the temporal sequences could be sketched as follows:

Past:
Origins of Toñita. She disappears. (Part II)

Future:
Death of Toñita. Anselmo's grief. (Parts II, III)

Present:
Anselmo's passion for Toñita. Life in the Tower (Part IV)

Present (cont'd):
A missing link: Toñita confinement and death. (Epilogue)

Anticipated Future:
Anselmo's confession. (Part IV)[14]

The same critic goes on to note that in spite of the greater complexity of the Anselmo-Toñita episode, the similarity with *Tirant lo Blanc* is striking. Not only do the two love stories follow "identical courses of temporal dislocation, but their elements (the erotic-lyrical, mysterious and secretive connotations) also have a strange resemblance. One wonders if Vargas Llosa had the 'Bodas Sordas' episode in mind when he wrote this part of *La Casa Verde.*"[15]

Besides the montage involved in the juxtaposition past-future-present-past, *The Green House* also relies on the montage of versions of the same story for the composition of the whole narrative. Vargas Llosa has said that one of the purposes of his techniques of the "Chinese boxes" and the "communicating vessels" is to expose the many sides of a given fragment of reality so as to exhaust the totality of its possibilities. The author of *The Green House* has compared the results of this procedure to a multifaceted geometrical form: the polyhedron. Within this analogy each episode could be conceived of as having planes of content and form. Following Vargas Llosa's analogy, we must then assume that each plane has the same size and number of sides as the other, and yet that it is different because it fits into a different location or contains different narrative materials. Vargas Llosa's use of the polyhedron as narrative strategy entails a criss-crossing play of the contents and forms of each plane. Thus, the polyhedron could be reconstituted into an ever-changing object. This analogy is not far from the idea behind a kaleidoscope. The number of permutations, though exhaustive of the colors first introduced in the mechanism, is, however, finite and rather limited.

Vargas Llosa's use of the fragment may be seen as a device to exhaust the diversity of what he calls reality. Another of his now famous narrative stratagems is the telescopic conversation in narrative. One character, let us say Jum, tells Aquilino his life story. The people who figure in Jum's story in turn tell Aquilino or another character in another time frame their own life story. This procedure can be reproduced ad infinitum. It constitutes the mainstay of *The Green House*'s narrative movement. Fushía's story is almost entirely related in this fashion. As he journeys downriver on Aquilino's boat, Fushía reminisces. Sadly, trying to order and understand the past events that now constitute his life, he talks. From time to time he responds to Aquilino's questions, offering information that clarifies ambiguous past sequences or confusing motivation. In this manner Fushía, as well as the other character-narrators, offers conflicting and even contradictory information. Each person tells the story from his or her *flawed,* insufficient and self-motivated point of view, producing an enormous sense of ambiguity in the novel.

Because so many factors in the narrative technique outlined above can be pinpointed in Fushía's version of his two escapes (from Brazil and from the island), this segment of *The Green House* has become a classic illustration of the telescopic conversation-storytelling device. Perhaps to entertain him or to lift Fushía's deepening depression, Aquilino asks the sick man to tell him once more how he escaped from prison. The story plunges deep into the past, before World War II in Brazil, when Fushía was a mere adolescent:

> "I'll just stay here where I am," Fushía said. "I can feel a chill and my whole body is shaking."
>
> "O.K., anything that makes you feel better. Come

> on, tell me once and for all how did you escape? What did they have you in for? How old were you?"
>
> He was going to school and that is why the Turk gave him a job in his warehouse. He kept accounts, Aquilino, in big books labelled Debits and Credits. And even though he was honest then, he was already dreaming of becoming a rich man. How he used to save, old man. He only ate one meal a day, no cigarettes, no drinking. He wanted to have a little capital and get into business. But that is life, the Turk got it into his head that he was stealing from him, all lies, and he had him sent to jail.
>
> "But you already told me that when we left the Island, Fushía," Aquilino said. "I want you to tell me how you escaped."
>
> "With this picklock," Chango said. Iricuo made it with wire from the cot.
>
> We tried it out, it opens the door without making any noise. Do you want to see, Jappy? (28–29).

In this quotation we see a third, absent person, Chango, responding to Aquilino's question. It is as if Fushía did not want to bother with this detail of the escape, and so his consciousness puts forth Chango's "unmediated" but past speech act. Chango provides the mechanical details of the escape, which in the light of Fushía's previous self-exculpation from any crime have to be interpreted as the romantic jail escape of the innocently incarcerated.

While in this example the interpolation of a third narrator or witness contributes important information and thus clarifies the previously shadowy nature of the event in question, there are many instances of telescopic conversations in *The Green House* in which initial confusion grows a great deal more before it is clarified by the storytellers' several subsequent interpolations. With the following example we have an illustration of the device of telescopic conversations employed to a critical limit. Three simultaneous conversations are recorded in this sequence, rescuing yet another scene from Fushía's halcyon days:

> "Good luck, you mean," Aquilino said.... "By the way Fushía, why did you have to fight with Mr. Reátegui? You must have really done it to him."
>
> He pulled a few good ones on him, and the first one was right after he arrived in Iquitos, he didn't even know him then, old man. He told him about it much later and Reátegui himself had a good laugh, oh, so you were the one who put the squeeze on Don Fabio, and Aquilino, Don Fabio, the governor of Santa María de Nieva?
>
> "At your service, Sir," Don Fabio said. "What can I do for you, will you stay long in Iquitos?"
>
> He planned to stay for a long time, maybe indefinitely. The lumber business, did he know? He was going to set up a sawmill near Nauta and he was expecting some engineers. He had fallen behind in his work, he could pay some more, but he wanted a large, comfortable room and Don Fabio, of course, of course, he was at his service, old man: he swallowed it hook, line, and sinker.
>
> "He gave me the best one in the entire hotel," Fushía said. It had windows facing the jipipapas garden....
>
> "Wasn't Reátegui in Iquitos?" Aquilino said. "Was he rich then?"
>
> "No, he became rich later, with the contraband," Fushía said. "But he already owned that little hotel, and he had begun trading with the Indian tribes....

He bought rubber, skins, and he sold them in Iquitos. That was when I got the idea, Aquilino. But, the same problem always, you need capital and I didn't have a red cent."

"And did you get away with a lot of money, Fushía?" Aquilino asked.

"Five thousand soles, Don Julio," Don Fabio said. "And my passport, and some silverware. . . . But I'll make it up to you, I swear it, with the sweat of my brow, Don Julio, to the last cent."

"Have you ever had any regrets, Fushía?" Aquilino said. "I've been meaning to ask you that for a long, long time."

"Regrets, for robbing that bastard Reátegui?" Fushía said. "He is rich only because he stole more than me, old man. . . ."

"And what good is your head then?" Don Julio Reátegui said. "How come it didn't even occur to you to ask him for his papers, Don Fabio?"

But he had asked for them and his passport looked brand new, how was he to know that it was forged, Don Julio? (49–50).

One of the effects of telescopic conversations is to place the entire flow of the novel on a double spiral. Time and space are thus distributed in each scene or segment over two strands, but these strands do not merely duplicate each other; rather, they modify one another. The fact that Fushía and Don Fabio, in response to Aquilino's questions, tell the story of Fushía's theft and false identity in Iquitos seems to heighten the veracity of the story at the same time that it provides the ethical value of Fushía's acts with a double prism.

It is indeed true that Vargas Llosa's stated purpose

of exhausting reality by presenting the same event from different points of view, reviewed by the consciousness of various participants, does confer upon the story of *The Green House* a certain thickness that the strictly linear development of the plot could not afford. But precisely because each scene, event, and episode is subject to the procedure of numerous cinematic takes, an individual character's own authority is reduced to a mere perspective among others. The life stories of Fushía, Lalita, Lituma, Bonifacia, Jum, inasmuch as they are autobiographies, seem reduced to the status of fabrication or speculation. No matter how much memory, fantasy, dreams, myth, magic, or even history is woven together in the characters' portrait, lives nevertheless, appear dispersed and alienated from the very persons who live the experience. In the end none of the takes is endowed with greater authority than the others. A movable ambiguity is set in circulation throughout the novel. Things and events are never unequivocal. Reality seems made up of the characters' self-deception, half-truths, lies, and, especially in the case of Fushía and Anselmo, an incommensurate fanciful desire. Revelation for the characters and interpretation for the reader remain difficult, refractory quests.

In *The Green House* a narrative structure based on apparent chaos, multiplicity of narrators and events, displacement of chronology, discontinuity in space, characters' double identities, and sudden shifts in the enunciation eventually produces a thematic presence which mirrors the narrative rhetoric. In the end, we read novels because they create the illusion of a world in which we recognize, modify, or refresh our understanding and feeling for life as we experience or imagine it. Life in *The Green House* appears fraught with uncertainty, anxiety, cruelty, and alienation. Daily life seems to be a current of endless and meaningless change. Such change entails duplicity, oppression, enslavement, and above all the inescapable reality of constant pain in a pressing struggle to survive.

NOTES

1. "Una insurrección permanente," *Marcha* 4 Mar. 1966; quoted from Mario Vargas Llosa, *Contra viento y marea* (Barcelona: Seix Barral, 1983) 86.

2. "La literatura es fuego," originally published in *Mundo Nuevo* 12 Aug. 1967: 93–95. Quoted here from *Contra viento y marea* 132.

3. *Contra viento y marea* 134.

4. *Antología Mínima de Mario Vargas Llosa* (Buenos Aires: Editorial Tiempo Contemporáneo, 1969).

5. *Antología Mínima* 14–15.

6. *Antología Mínima* 26–27.

7. Mario Vargas Llosa, *historia secreta de una novela* (Barcelona: Tusquets, 1971) 50. This and all subsequent translations are mine.

8. *Historia secreta* 54–55. I have not been able to identify this reference in the Library of Congress catalogues.

9. *Historia secreta* 62.

10. Dick Gerdes, *Mario Vargas Llosa* (Boston: Twayne, 1985) 58.

11. Gerdes 63.

12. Mario Vargas Llosa, *La casa verde* (Barcelona: Seix Barral, 1965) 9. All quotations are taken from the 12th edition (1972). Page numbers are indicated parenthetically. These are my translations.

13. Mario Vargas Llosa, "Carta de batalla por *Tirant lo Blanc,*" *Tirant lo Blanc* (Madrid: Alianza Editorial, 1969) 465.

14. Luis A. Diez, *Mario Vargas Llosa's Pursuit of the Total Novel* (Cuernavaca: CIDOC, 1970) 449–50.

15. Diez 450.

CHAPTER FOUR

Conversation in The Cathedral: Descent into Hell

Between *The Green House* and *Conversation in The Cathedral,* Vargas Llosa published his only short novel, *Los cachorros* (1967 [*The Cubs,* 1978]). In this technically flawless narrative he revisits once more the social milieu of the suburb of Miraflores and the dilemmas and anxieties of the upper-class male adolescent. The story of *The Cubs* is fashioned around a newspaper account of a boy's tragedy: a dog castrated him in a freak encounter. In the tight space of this short novel Vargas Llosa marshals with great economy many of the narrative devices employed in his two earlier long novels. In *The Cubs* all narrative material stands in equilibrium. The result is a masterpiece in which a great many of the thematic obsessions found in *The Time of the Hero*—anxiety, rites of passage, sexual fantasy, codes of machismo—are recombined with new poignancy.

The Cubs was followed by the enormous two-volume (699 pages) *Conversation in The Cathedral.* In this multiple tale of evil and sadistic pleasure Vargas Llosa brings all his technical creative might to a culminating point. His narrative style would seem to have congealed into a unique set of artistic choices easily recognizable as his own. This novel is an exhaustive and overwhelming inquiry into the nature and dynamics of evil in relation to a power that corrupts absolutely. It is considered by many critics to be Vargas Llosa's most pessimistic as well as his most deeply reflective text. The novel marks a new level of artistic maturity in the meteoric career of a writer who in 1969 was barely thirty-three years old.

In this demonstration of virtuosity critics have documented the influences of Faulkner, Joyce, Dos Passos, and Hemingway. Because the novel brings its major character, Santiago Zavala, to the most abject levels of depression, disenchantment, and cynicism, some critics have seen it as a culmination of modernist ideology. Quoting from Kinsley Widmer, Dick Gerdes writes that in *Conversation in The Cathedral* the sense of life as a sordid and meaningless series of contradictions parallels "Dostoyevsky's outrageous paradoxes, Conrad's nihilistic fears, Lawrence's apocalyptic yearnings, Hemingway's *nada,* Faulkner's puritan fears, Celine's journeyings, Wright's black quilts, and the West's surreal mockeries.[1]

In *Conversation in The Cathedral* the adolescents from the military academy and the young men from *The Cubs* have become university students. These young men—and women—have passed the tests and rites of initiation. They consider themselves autonomous, mature individuals responsible for themselves and for the future of their country. No longer isolated within the confines of the military academy or their neighborhood, they plunge into university life, defined by one of the characters as a microcosm of Peruvian political life. While the novel takes university life as the point of departure for the story, the total narrative breadth of *Conversation in The Cathedral* extends deeply and widely into other sectors and periods of Peru's social fabric. The plot chronicles the years of the Odría dictatorship (1948–56) and the disastrous effects that this oppressive and corrupt regime had on Peruvian society as a whole. Directly—with the planning of a student-labor uprising—or indirectly—in the conversation of politicians, maids, prostitutes, and journalists—the novel's discourse is centered on the question and dynamics of power. *Conversation in The Cathedral* is a political novel, and in many ways it can be seen now as the first installment of a tripartite historical inquiry into the nature of social and political change in Latin America. *The War of the End of the World* and *The Real Story of Alejandro Mayta* could be considered the second and third parts of the triptych.

From Characters and Story to Plot

Vargas Llosa brings together over one hundred characters in *Conversation in The Cathedral.* The total effect of the narrative's complexity has been compared to a whirlwind. In many ways it is reminiscent of Sartre's *The Reprieve,* the novel in which the French writer portrays the anguish of his characters on the eve of France's plunge into the Second World War.[2] Although Vargas Llosa's novel juxtaposes almost twenty separate conversations, the story is confined to the results of the framing conversation between Santiago Zavala, a journalist, and Ambrosio Pardo, a dogcatcher and executioner. In the four-hour conversation between Santiago and his former chauffeur Ambrosio in a dingy, smelly, little pub called La Catedral, the life of both interlocutors is examined in a baroque retrospective. Each bit of information branches out into a different and unexpected avenue that in turn doubles back, only to branch out in yet another direction. The story lines intersect and intertwine in pursuit of two questions proposed by Santiago Zavala. On the surface of his detectivelike inquiry into Ambrosio's memory and consciousness, Santiago seeks an answer to the identity and motivation of La Musa's killer. At a deeper level Santiago seeks to know when and how his life and his country disintegrated.

The entire story is set in a sweeping retrospective movement. Once the novel localizes Santiago's late adolescence in his memory, through the scene in which he and his friends attempt to seduce Amalia, the story progresses directly to the moment when Santiago learns of his father's secret sexual identity. Although the novel's dualistic rhetoric suggests that the story is as much Ambrosio's as it is Santiago's, the undisputed center of the novel is Santiago: the novel's quest to know is predicated upon the parameters of Santiago's desire and consciousness. Santiago's quest is privileged above the consciousness of the other major and minor characters in that his consciousness is treated through a process of interior duplication, or *mise en abyme*. Santiago is the consciousness of the person who acted and lived before the revelation. Zavalita is the cynical, fallen consciousness who now understands, mocks, and commiserates with Santiago. As in Carlos Fuentes's *The Death of Artemio Cruz,* this divided interiority engages into a dialogic relationship with the past. On the one hand, the past is enunciated by the pronoun "I," or Santiago; on the other hand, a present is inscribed in the pronoun "you," or Zavalita. Such alienated interiority would seem to allude to Roland Barthes's famous structural binome in *S/Z*.

This interior duplication, or rather alienation, is not visible in Ambrosio, whose consciousness is not at all reflective. When the two men sit to drink and talk, the ensuing dialogue involves more than two sites of consciousness. It is a dialogue in three voices. Painful registers of the conversation in The Cathedral thus alternate with the sharpness of the lived moment (Ambrosio/Santiago), as well as the poignancy of the present light of illusion and disillusionment shining upon the innocent past (Santiago/Zavalita). Santiago and Ambrosio order, touch, sense the immanence of the past. Zavalita, from a distance, is revolted by his new understanding of the actions that Santiago and Ambrosio evoke. Zavalita asks for details and motives that in retrospect acquire determining importance. Ambrosio grows frustrated with these questions, for he remembers the past, unaffected by Zavalita's sense of revelation and new meanings. Unaware that he is actually speaking to two "men"—Santiago/Zavalita—Ambrosio grows weary of the motivated questioning. The chauffeur is often tempted to leave in order to end a casual conversation that has inadvertently become an inquisition. Finally, and ironically for the reader, he tells Santiago to let him alone and just plain go to hell. The dogcatcher does not want to answer any more of the journalist's questions, nor does he commune with Santiago's need to pile guilt on his father, Ambrosio's former and revered employer.

Santiago Zavala's journey traces the steps of a well-to-do young man caught in an identity crisis that also constitutes a historical crisis for his class. The genesis of this crisis is not fully examined in the novel, but the derogatory comments made by other characters upon Santiago's squeamishness regarding his family's wealth, ideology, and privileged position in Peruvian society indicate that the root of Santiago's conflicted views can be traced to his ample love for reading. Both his older brother, Chispas, and his sister, Teté, mock his book knowledge. Every time Santiago speaks to disagree with them, to offer an alternative interpretation of Peru's problems, they dismiss him, reminding him that his family nickname is *El Supersabio* (Mr. Know-it-all). The origin of Santiago's individual crisis and rebellion against the world of his parents is not expressly detailed as antecedent to his decision to enter San Marcos instead of the upper-class Catholic university. Instead the vivid canvas of desolate and pervasive corruption that the novel depicts as Peruvian society provides the terms and reasons for Santiago's ringing rejection of the status quo.

The favorite son of a wealthy upper-class family, Santiago is expected to enter a profession and follow a life style that will reproduce, in his generation, the values and privileges that his predecessors have obtained. Chispa, Santiago's older brother, is the embodiment of such choices. Affable, satisfied with life as it is, Chispas makes all the necessary decisions to ensure the continued future success and succession of the Zavala family. He learns to manage his father's pharmaceutical factories and to deal with the ever more demanding labor force, just as he learns to cope with a voracious military government. Above all Chispas exercises a very prudent choice of friends and associates. Toward all those Peruvians who do not belong to his small privileged class he displays the benevolent paternalism of his father. Neither Chispas nor Don Fermín ever appear as cruel, arrogant, or oppressive men. It is Doña Zoila who expresses and practices the rationale for strict class distinctions, the fear and anxiety of demeaning "race" mixtures, the phobia about the rabble, the *cholos*. The matron in the Zavala family reacts angrily, suffers, and bears all of Santiago's rebellious acts. She sees in each and every one of them a danger to the entire family. In Doña Zoila's strict differential code between *gente decente* and *cholos* (largely people of mixed Indian and Spanish descent), the slightest mistake can prove to be fatal. As far as she is concerned, Santiago not only holds the wrong values—concern for the entire national destiny—but he also associates with the wrong people, cavorts with the wrong ideas, and above all uses unbearably frank language. In the end, Doña Zoila is proven correct. In rebelling against his class, her son joins the ranks of the dreaded *cholos*. She is often softened into tolerance of Santiago's youthful mistakes by the easy-going Don Fermín. But when it comes to marriage, even Don Fermín agrees that the rules have to be enforced inflexibly; for marriage is the arena of life-or-death struggle for the maintenance of distinct and scarce privileges. Doña Zoila's worst fears become reality when Santiago, in a supreme act of rejection and dejection, marries his nurse, a sweet, superficial, nondescript, lower-class, nonwhite girl. Against Don

Fermín's willingness to forgive his beloved son once more, Doña Zoila lays down the law; Santiago and his wife must be socially excluded.

Santiago's transformation into Zavalita passes through three main knots. In defiance of his father's desire and his mother's counsel, Santiago chooses to enter San Marcos University, the old, once venerable national university where all aspirant classes of Peruvians seek the opportunity to improve their lot in life. There Santiago makes friends with an activist communist group. These young people, the Cahuide group, have read Marx and many other socialist thinkers. The members of the Cahuide group, as well as those of various other university groups, think that only a Marxist revolution will enable them and the majority of Peruvians to capture the state, make "the revolution," and set the nation once and for all on a road of development and justice.

At this juncture in the story it is clear that Santiago's desire to be part of the Cahuide group is plagued with tensions and contradictions. Santiago would like to be an activist but has no clear convictions; he acts like an activist only when guided and tutored by Aída. He is in fact an aesthetic dilettante whose inclinations are actually irreconcilable with the praxis and goals of the Cahuide group. Santiago falls in love with Aída, an articulate and committed member of the group. She humors him in friendship and in his interest in the group's readings and ideology, but never fails to remind him that he will never cease to be a bourgeois. Aída and Jacobo, the undisputed political and intellectual leader of the group, mock Santiago's enthusiasm for his idea of being a pure revolutionary dedicated to books and museums. As the group prepares to secretly join a student-worker rebellion against the dictatorship, they meet to count heads and to make final commitments. Santiago knows that the group perceives his doubts, that they will probably vote to expel him, and that Aída will side with Jacobo, the Jewish intellectual. Jacobo's and Aída's precise eye contact indicates that they are more than *camaradas,* and that to them Santiago, the friendly dilettante, is not really important enough to expel. The group reluctantly assigns him a minor role in the final plans for the uprising.

Having failed to win Aída, and ruminating on his doubts, Santiago goes through the motions of playing his assigned part. He is unaware, though, that because the dictator's regime suspects his father of betraying the regime by joining in a new alliance of rich men against General Odría, he too has been under surveillance, and the Zavala family phone has been tapped. The Cahuide group is thus arrested minutes before their moment of "glory." Santiago spends a few happy hours under arrest together with the group. Soon his father, making use of his connections in high places, especially his friendship with Cayo Bermúdez, chief of secret police, obtains Santiago's release.

His father's gift of freedom is regarded by Santiago as the final affront his family could inflict upon him, and he decides to break openly with them. The Cahuide group is forever forgotten. Santiago never makes any attempt to help them out of jail nor to find out what happened to any of them. Refusing his family's help, he goes to live with a renegade bohemian uncle who eventually finds him a job on one of the city's tabloids, *La Crónica*. Santiago's writing skills are quickly recognized, and he is assigned to reporting crime news under the guidance of the old, famed, and crusty Becerrita. The Prado family, one of the richest, most influential, and staunchest supporters of the dictatorial regime, own the newspaper. Doña Zoila would have more than approved marriage into this family, members of the Peruvian aristocracy. Eventually, and ironically, Santiago marries a sweet *cholita* whom he meets in a clinic where he has to go for a minor operation. The antics of elopement of Santiago and his wife-to-be foreshadow Marito and Julia's elopement in *La tía Julia y el escribidor*.

After a few months of a dull honeymoon, Santiago settles into his job and into full depression. However, the boredom, disorientation, solitude, and sadness of his routine are to be shattered into dejection and self-pity when Santiago, performing a routine investigation of the murder of Lima's most coveted whore, La Musa, finds out that his father is in fact the famed homosexual Bola de Oro.

On the main trunk of Santiago's story, the reader can see knots for the branching stories of Amalia, Cayo Bermúdez, Don Fermín, Queta, La Musa, Becerrita, Carlos, and Ambrosio Pardo. The whirlwind created by the conversational structure of the narrative can be stopped and recomposed in the reader's memory into a series of simultaneous, yet linear, individual stories. Each story devolves upon a major character. By means of the conversational structure each character tells the bulk of his or her own story, with the exception of Cayo Bermúdez, who is mostly seen from a variety of angles but at a distance. While Zavalita's crisis is extensively detailed and richly embroidered by the internal alienation produced by the split between I and Thou, Cayo Bermúdez's passions and motivations remain dark, secret, unfathomable.

Amalia, the good-looking, simple-minded immigrant from the highlands to Lima, proves to be a key character in the weaving of the novel's story. While Santiago is the central consciousness and character in *Conversation in The Cathedral,* the comprehensive story line demands that certain characters shuffle between the different and quite separate spheres of Peruvian life represented on the huge canvas of the novel. In keeping with the realistic tenor of the novel's mimesis, Santiago's coherence as a "pure," sheltered, upper-class young rebel would be seriously damaged if he were to visit the whorehouses, Cayo's "home," his father's apartment in Ancón, the worker's political meetings, or the shantytowns in the outskirts of Lima or Pucallpa. Other characters, whose experiences provide the "reasons" for Santiago's radical dissatisfaction with and critique of the world, live the realities of the uprising in Arequipa, factory work, and prostitution. Santiago has access to these worlds by means of two key characters, Ambrosio and Amalia. As servants, these two loyal, humble, displaced individuals circulate freely through the many separate spheres of the society portrayed in the novel.

Amalia and Ambrosio are keen but prudent observers of the behavior of their masters. They know that their masters do everything differently from them, so they struggle to deliver their services exactly as they understand their orders, never judging or questioning these orders nor the desires of the master. In this sense

Amalia and Ambrosio play a role similar to the dumb eye of a camera. But of course such objectivity is not possible. If Amalia, for instance, does not realize at first that La Musa is Cayo's kept woman, she can tell that the home furnishings are expensive, that the couple spend more time drinking liquor than doing anything else, that they sleep during the day and party at night, and that when Queta visits, she is often received in bed. None of this "objective" information is, of course, value free. While Amalia may not come to any conclusions, the reader certainly receives and reconstructs the coded information masquerading as free, objective, observation.

Amalia's story is simple and tragic. She first appears in the employ of the Zavala family. There she serves Santiago and meets Ambrosio, who is currently the family's chauffeur. One afternoon Santiago and his high school chums try to drug and rape her. She is blamed for the affair and dismissed. Later paternalistic Don Fermín gives her a job in one of his pharmaceutical factories. There she meets Trinidad, a half-crazed Aprista party worker. Eventually, after much courting, she agrees to become his concubine. They live in one of Lima's filthy shantytowns. Trinidad suffers from delirium tremens as a result of either previous torture in prison or drinking. He dies. Amalia then finds a job at La Musa's home, thanks to Ambrosio. There she again meets Ambrosio, now working as Cayo Bermúdez's chauffeur and bodyguard.

Ambrosio's earlier attraction to Amalia is now obvious to her. She is puzzled by his apparently new affection for her. She does not understand his previous indifference at the Zavala household. During one of their many conversations Ambrosio tells her that he already loved her when they served at the Zavalas, but that his respect for Don Fermín kept him from showing any interest in her.

When La Musa's good fortune suddenly turns sour, Amalia, the faithful servant, follows her. Living in a little apartment with practically no money and with a drugged, crazed mistress, Amalia continues to date Ambrosio. One day La Musa is killed. Amalia flees. She accidentally stumbles into Ambrosio, who had been searching for her. He tells her to make ready, that they are moving to a place in the jungle, Pucallpa, and getting married. She follows Ambrosio, and in Pucallpa they settle down humbly but happily. While he tries to start his own trucking service, she dies in childbirth.

After Amalia's death, and after being swindled by the man who sold the truck, Ambrosio moves back to Lima. His story is long and complex. It reaches back into the life of the rural coastal communities of Peru. Recently Gregorio Martínez, another Peruvian novelist, has written several narratives (*Tierra de Caléndula,* 1975, and *Canto de sirena,* 1977) that delve deeply and with extraordinary insight into the life of the descendants of black slaves, the Indian peoples, and their Spanish masters in the southern Peruvian areas of Chincha and Ica. While Amalia's past in the high Andes is taken as given, Ambrosio's childhood as a poor mulatto boy in a class- and race-conscious society is richly portrayed. Ambrosio's own memorial about his early years in Chincha plays a double function in the novel, for he was then an acquaintance of Cayo Bermúdez.

To be exact, Ambrosio is not really a mulatto. His last name accurately depicts his racial status in Peruvian society. He is *pardo,* a man of Indian and African descent, culturally part of the black stratum in coastal societies of Peru. Living in the same town, sharing with him in games and childhood adventures, Cayo Bermúdez is also a dark man of humble social and economic means, but his is not black. While Ambrosio remains economically and socially within the limits of his class and race, Cayo Bermúdez's father makes a small fortune. Cayo turns out to be a brilliant fellow with a superb future ahead of him. But against his father's hopes and wishes, as if to spite all the social codes and mores in the world, Cayo not only falls in love with a beautiful black girl but insists on marrying her. This intolerable violation of the most sacred space—marriage—produces the irreconcilable estrangement between Cayo and his father. Like Santiago's, Cayo's resolve will not bend. He and his wife move to a shabby little house on the outskirts of town. Then, Cayo settles into obscurity, never heard from again until the day when Ambrosio sees him in downtown Lima as chief of the secret police and an acquaintance of Ambrosio's rich and influential boss, Don Fermín Zavala.

In the novel both Ambrosio and Amalia provide access to the life of the lower classes by virtue of their own self-awareness and experiences, and also by playing the roles of go-betweens. They conjugate Santiago's self-enclosure of privilege with the hell lived by the other characters in the novel. Ironically, Ambrosio, as chauffeur to two powerful and corrupt men, shuffles between the sites of their domestic and public acts.

Ambrosio witnesses the family's tensions as well as the political crisis that Don Fermín and Don Cayo have to face and surmount. Almost always silent and invisible to his bosses, the black chauffeur is aware of all their frustrations, pain, and solitude. Eventually he identifies with their personal struggles and their dejected solitude in the back seat of the cars he drives. Ambrosio's compassion toward the two father figures (Don Fermín and Cayo's father, Trifulcio) stands in stark contrast with Santiago's rage, implacable accusations, and utter dejection.

Cut out to fit the profile of the stereotypical black slave, Ambrosio has physical qualities that make him an overgrown member of the human species. He is big but cowardly (although he murders); he is vexed but compassionate; he is uneducated but highly civilized; he is humble and oppressed but loyal to his oppressors; he is physically and ideologically heterosexual but more than permissive toward his former master's homosexuality; he is ideologically conscious of his blackness but desires a mulatto woman with the same fetishism (and ideological desire) of a nonblack male. Some critics of *Conversation in The Cathedral,* focusing particularly on Ambrosio's emphasized passivity and cowardliness, have found his alleged murder of La Musa incoherent.

Ambrosio's linear journey takes him from his hot and dry village to the Lima dog pound. In between, he serves as Don Fermín's chauffeur, then as Don Cayo's chauffeur, and later as Don Cayo's chauffeur and bodyguard. He also becomes Don Fermín's semiconsenting homosexual lover, falls in love with Amalia, marries her, and perhaps, murders La Musa.

His trajectory touches on the mysteries and secrets of all the major characters' lives. This is the reason why Santiago talks to him, peppering him with questions. Not unlike the Greek sphinx, Ambrosio seems unmoved by Santiago's assumption that he holds the answer to the riddle. Ambrosio is willing to tell, but he will tell it in his own way, paying attention to what is important to him, in feigned disregard for Santiago's obsessions and anxieties. If Santiago is smart enough to select items and put them together into an answer, that too is fine with Ambrosio. Thus, the huge black man emerges as a doubly passive figure. His memory is not motivated by an intelligent consciousness; his acts are not spurred by specific driving desires. His wealth of information and his life appear to be drifting, disconnected from any project of his own. The only two expectations in his life would seem to have been his desire to sleep with Queta and his love for Amalia.

Ambrosio's dispassionate and unmotivated consciousness is, of course, essential to the novel's rhetorical narrative style, for Ambrosio's seemingly indifferent yet plentiful memory allows Santiago's detection activity and the novel as a whole to create the illusion of a mystery plot. The distance between the silent Cayo, the merrily laughing Musa, the swearing Queta, and Santiago's perception of them is partly the result of the fact that these underworld characters are generally placed from within Ambrosio's or Amalia's apparently flat vision.

Don Cayo Bermúdez moves from the obscurity of his provincial town life to the penumbra of his hellish and secretive empire by pure accident. He happens to have been a chum of one of the military commanders now empowered by General Odría's dictatorship. Though Cayo's consciousness is almost always presented in reverie, it would seem that his instant willingness to accept the job as head of secret police is a desire to inhabit the dark chambers of power.

In one way or another, all the characters in *Conversation in The Cathedral* meet their doom during the dictatorship's eight years. Don Cayo is the single exception. The protest riots of Arequipa, which shake the regime to its foundations and demand Don Cayo's resignation, prove in the end to be a mere accident for which the chief of secret police had been well prepared. Don Cayo had coldly and rationally anticipated his downfall. He never fooled himself into thinking that the Odría crowd were his friends, much less, of course, the businessmen and aristocrats who buttered him up and sought his favor. Don Cayo is consistently and cynically conscious that his lot in politics is to do the dirty jobs that keep the general and his allied bourgeoisie in power. This knowledge is the source of his power. He seeks no moral justification for his evildoing. He makes no attempt to disguise, in patriotic or class interest terms, the nature of his infernal métier. Knowing that at any moment he can be used as the scapegoat for the regime's corruption, Don Cayo has been putting money away in foreign banks. When the Arequipa revolts take the upper hand in the arena of national politics, he takes a plane and leaves the country. Years later, when the military regime has been forgotten, and in comparison with the torpor and chaos of the current (current to the time of Santiago's and Ambrosio's conversation) civilian rulers, it actually looks good that Don Cayo should return to Peru. He can now peacefully enjoy the result of his successful finances. Upon his return, he has no misgivings. The past is done and over with. Unlike Santiago, the former chief of secret police is not curious about anyone else's destiny, whether good, bad, or indifferent. Such steadiness in the face of pain, injustice, and murder confirms the suspicion that Don Cayo's amatory relationship with La Musa was purely instrumental.

Santiago learns that Don Cayo Bermúdez is cultivated by his father, a senator in the dictator's mock parliament. Don Cayo invites several other gentlemen of the old school to his home, where La Musa plays the role of hostess and lover. In the evenings at Don Cayo's the gentlemen are tempted by, and gladly succumb to, the feminine charms of La Musa and her lover, the famed *mulata* Queta. In their more intimate hours Don Cayo indulges in the voyeuristic pleasure of watching La Musa and Queta make love at his command. Don Cayo also discovers that Don Fermín's well-disguised repugnance at Queta's or La Musa's advances are in fact motivated by his homosexual preferences. Very obligingly Cayo procures him his chauffeur, Ambrosio, to satisfy the senator's tormented desires. Santiago learns that Queta's version of La Musa's murder is probably true: Ambrosio killed her in order to deliver Don Fermín/Bola de Oro from further scandal and blackmail.

Narrative Structure

The sheer length, complexity of plot, and character motivation of *Conversation in The Cathedral* place new demands on the reader's memory and attention. For instance, it takes some acumen to figure out just when, in the course of all the interconnected events, La Musa was killed. Just as Santiago finds incredible the idea of his father's being the legendary Bola de Oro, the reader has difficulties making this same identification because information comes in bits and pieces, glimpses of scenes, and tails of gossipy conversations.

Although the entire narrative is constituted out of the ongoing conversation between Santiago and Ambrosio the narrative body and density of the novel entail the montage effect of nineteen conversations superimposed on each other. As we saw in *The Green House,* one dialogue contains another dialogue that in turn contains another dialogue, and so on. Each dialogue evolves a different set of characters speaking from different points in space and time. Similarly *Conversation in The Cathedral* involves, at times, six simultaneous conversations within the original outer frame. Vargas Llosa's own description of the Chinese box set-up would seem most applicable here but only partially. In the Chinese box what one encounters inside the first large box are other boxes that merely duplicate and repeat the same design of the outer frame. However, Vargas Llosa's set-up of conversation within conversation, provides for diversity, variation, and a great deal of branching out from the main topics driving the originating conversation.

As we earlier noted in Fushía's recollection of his escape from prison in Brazil, in Ambrosio or Santiago's recollection other voices intervene to tell their version or contribute their information to Santiago's incomplete vision of the event chronicled. For instance, the Arequipa revolt is told in a conversation between

Ludovico and Ambrosio, which is itself placed within Santiago and Ambrosio's ongoing conversation. But inside the Ludovico-Ambrosio dialogue Hipólito, another participant and eyewitness to the Arequipa revolt, tells his version of the riveting adventure too:

> "It was about time, Ambrosio," Ludovico said. "All it takes is for a man to be down, and his friends disappear."
>
> "Do you think I would not have come to see you before?" Ambrosio asked. "I only found out this morning, Ludovico, and that's only because I met Hipólito."
>
> "That son of a bitch told you?" Ludovico said. "But I bet he didn't tell you everything."
>
> "What is all this about Ludovico, what happened?" Ambrosio said. "A whole month since he left for Arequipa, and not a word."
>
> "He is all wrapped up, from head to toe at the Police Forces Hospital," Hipólito said.
>
> "The boys in Arequipa made minced meat out of him."[3]

The semiomniscient narrator takes over the triple conversational set, and adopting Trifulcio's (Ambrosio's father's) point of view begins to narrate the events of the day when the government's heavy strikebreakers left for Arequipa. Still from Trifulcio's point of view, the narrator sets up a bridge to get back to the opening conversation between Ambrosio and Ludovico, but this time their conversation will include Téllez's part of the story:

> He did not feel well, his whole body hurt. O.K., ready, on to Arequipa, said the man who gave the orders. And the truck left.

"Dislocations, bruises, hemorrhages," Ludovico said. "When the doctor comes to see me, he gives me some medicine. These are fucking days, Ambrosio."

"Amalia and I were remembering, just last Sunday," Ambrosio said, "that you didn't feel like going to Arequipa."

"Now at least I can sleep," Ludovico said. "The first days, even my nails hurt, Ambrosio."

"But just think what luck," Ambrosio said, "You took a beating while in service and now they have to reward you."

"And who are those guys in the coalition?" Téllez said.

"Well, it was while in service and it was not, they sent us and they did not. You have no idea what kind of brothel politics is, Ambrosio."

"Let me tell you: they are a bunch of shitheads," the one who gave the order laughed, "and we are going to fuck up their demonstration."

"I was just asking, to have a conversation topic and make the trip more fun," Téllez said. "This is very boring" (2:120–21).

The novel relies heavily on mimesis of the conversational abilities of the characters it portrays. It is as if a character's lesser or greater development and importance depended on that same character's gift to verbalize the terms of his or her lived experience. In this context the text's exploitation of an autobiographical impulse confirms Lévi-Strauss's assertion that narration, or storytelling, is one of the first instances of the mind. We understand the world not only by means of the four primary Kantian categories—quality, quantity, relation, and modality—but also by means of the narrative equation in which agent, action, event, the I—Thou relation, cause and effect, and above all sensory perception are articulated in memory and language. Sensory perception would seem to be the screen through which all consciousness is portrayed in *Conversation in The Cathedral.*

By means of conversation Vargas Llosa not only narrates the action in a series of crisscrossing retrospective scenes, but he also delves into character complexity. In *Conversation in The Cathedral* the author portrays the myriad complexities and feel of Peru's social and racial class system caught in a silent and undetected process of decomposition. The dramatic and melodramatic experiences of Amalia, Santiago, La Musa, Cayo, Becerrita, and Carlitos announce a farewell to Doña Zoila's world. In interviews Vargas Llosa has detailed how very difficult the writing of this novel proved to be for him. Not only did he attempt to describe a very painful period of his own life and his generation, but also the sheer number of characters and their complexity grew to an intolerable level of possible combinations. Vargas Llosa has said of this period in Peruvian political life that it was a dictatorship that robbed his generation, for there were no heroes and no martyrs. The dictatorship produced only failures. José Miguel Oviedo believes that the writing of an openly political novel posed a special challenge to Vargas Llosa's own criteria of novelistic objectivity and impartiality. Oviedo writes that Vargas Llosa "would have to admit to the inevitable confrontation of his fictional elaboration with real and public models which were not confined to a single institution, as in *The Time of the Hero;* nor were they marginal, as in

The Green House; instead, they were widely known and easily identifiable to the national public.[4]

In this regard Vargas Llosa has said that he tried to be faithful to the historical period that his novel portrays: "When a writer attempts, in a book, to show certain social and historical aspects of life, he must be truthful. If he alludes to real events, he must do so honestly. That is what I try to do. For instance, right now I am writing a novel that takes place in Peru, between 1948 and 1956, and in my eagerness to document myself, I have even read the speeches of General Odría."[5]

However, Vargas Llosa's mimetic art does not rely on the direct incorporation of data he selects from his research. Whatever information he may gain from reading documents pertaining to the period he fictionalizes is rendered in the novelistic terms of his realism. For instance, the minutia of the conspiracy against the dictator and the violent events of the Arequipa revolt are rendered by Ludovico, Hipólito, and Trifulcio's personal testimonies, feelings, and memory. In *Conversation in The Cathedral,* individual memory constitutes the main source of information on the historical period that the novel's plot brings to life. The dictator, whose speeches Vargas Llosa took the trouble to read, does not appear in the novel. His person and his deeds can only be inferred through the acts of his henchman (Cayo Bermúdez), his ally (Don Fermín), and his victims (Jacobo, Santiago, Aída, Trinidad). Thus, the dictator appears less as a determining historical force and more as a product of a thoroughly corrupt and cynical society that reproduces itself regardless of the individual wills or projects.

The multiplicity of stories told in the novel creates an overwhelming sense of circularity. Each segment of each story provides new information that causes the plot line to inch forward. In the end, however, each story seems to connect with the beginning of yet another story set in a previous time frame. The juxtaposed telling of stories occurring at different points in the past creates a contrapuntal effect in plot. Yet the general energy of the plot moves constantly forward, so that out of the chaos of voices, fragments of scenes, and interrupted stories a schematic and direct line from Santiago's household to La Musa's murder emerges. The organization of so many different plot lines, all fragmented in order to produce the sense of a vortex, forces the reader to pay special attention to the names of the characters engaged in recollection and conversation. The names of the characters function, as in *The Green House,* as marks left behind to signal the direction of a tortuous trail cut in the thicket of an unknown forest.

In fact, the body of *Conversation in The Cathedral* is as carefully organized as Vargas Llosa's two previous novels. The novel has four sections of roughly equal length. Each part is focused on a major event in the plot and meaning of the story: 1) the awakening of Santiago's social and moral consciousness; 2) Hortensia/La Musa's settling in as Cayo's lover and hostess; 3) La Musa's murder; 4) the definitive closing in of Santiago's demoralized, self-deprecating consciousness.

In the unfolding of the plot characters are continuously arranged in tensed triangles that struggle over the possession and disclosure of a secret: 1) La Musa-

Queta-Cayo; 2) Santiago-Ambrosio-La Musa/Queta-Cayo; 3) Amalia-Queta-La Musa; 4) Ludovico-Hipólito-Trifulcio; 5) Queta-Becerrita-Santiago; 6) Jacobo-Aída-Santiago. These and other triangular sets of relations admit many other combinations. As the other possible combinations take place in the novel, the information, passions, fantasies, desires, and above all the sensory perception of the characters are set in an endless circulatory current that dynamizes the entire body of the novel's melodramatic happenings.

Santiago's Descent into Hell

As the novel draws to a close, a succession of brief dialogues between Santiago/Zavalita and the bohemian Carlitos take place at the Negro-Negro night club. Although Santiago's descent down the ladder to hell began long before this poignant set of scenes, the selection and the description of the Negro-Negro seems symbolic of Santiago's new state: he is a sadder though not wiser man. Lost, and sick to his stomach in the aftermath of Queta's revelation, Santiago accidentally meets Carlitos at the bus stop:

> He allowed himself to be dragged, as if sleepwalking he stepped down the narrow stairway of the Negro-Negro, blindly, he crossed stumbling over the empty darkness of the place, the usual table was free, two German beers, Carlitos told the waiter, and he leaned against the covers of The New Yorker.... There, the magazine covers always shiny, sardonic, and multicolored, the rumor of the conversations of the invisible customers. The waiter brought the beers, they both drank at the same time (2:35)

Carlitos tries to reason with Santiago's feelings. Yes, they are trapped; yes, the situation is hopeless. But there is no need for such masochism, argues the nihilistic Carlitos. Santiago's friend points out that Santiago's depression is due not so much to the knowledge he has gained about the identity of La Musa's murderer but rather to the blow Santiago's false pride has taken with the business about Bola de Oro: "The fucking thing is not the murder business, that has to be a lie, Zavalita, but your finding out, over there, about the other thing, and by way of such a mouth. I thought you already knew about it, Zavalita" (2:36). As if Zavalita could not hear Carlito's splitting hairs about Don Fermín's possible implication in a murder and his homosexuality, Santiago/Zavalita's mind wanders in the recesses of his split consciousness: "You repeated it once more, it could not be." As if in the background, Carlito's argument is barely registered in Santiago/Zavalita's drifting mind: "Zavalita, there are things even more terrible than that. You will get used to it, in time you won't give a fuck, and more beer" (2:36).

In *The Time of the Hero* "the truth" as the main problem of the novel takes on its real importance only in the epilogue. In *Conversation in The Cathedral* the constitution and meaning of "the truth" plays a dominant thematic role. Not for a minute can Santiago/Zavalita free himself from his search for "the truth." The damned truth comes forth with unrestrained force in the novel's discourse. All conversations testify to it and thus make it undeniable. There is no room for confusion or ambiguity in the confessional of *Conversation in The Cathedral.* But this truth, just as in *The Time of the Hero,* remains private and individualized;

it cannot break through the pact of self-censorship that the oppressed and suffering have contracted with their masters. Once Queta, outraged at la Musa's unpunished murder, musters the courage to spell it out, she discovers that nobody, not even Becerrita, will dare publish the truth. The ensuing reconstructed dialogue between Queta and the investigative reporter for *La Crónica* belies the entire fabric of the society in which Santiago/Zavalita and everyone else flounder:

Queta:	"Is he going to say it? Is he going to publish it?"
Becerrita:	"We are not going to splash everyone with shit."
Ivonne:	"Tell her what can happen if she continues repeating that story."
Queta:	"Coward, wretch, I knew that it was a waste, that you would not dare" (2:33–34).

Santiago, whose consciousness eventually bears the entire weight of the truth, pays, in a manner of speaking, with his life. He would be better off denying "the truth" he discovers. But such denial would prove to be, as in Carlito's case, just another form of self-destruction. The truth, as Becerrita admits, is too vast and too terrible to either repress, deny, or reveal. In all cases Bola de Oro's truth destroys all the illusions and pacts of the past. It can only be repressed and suppressed. Limbo is the only antidote against it. Thus, like "the truth" of the Slave's murder in *The Time of the Hero,* "the truth" in *Conversation in The Cathedral* is best filed in archives, destined to be forgotten. "The truth" becomes one more piece in the archives of what Sartre has called bad faith, because this truth, even though it was the true object of Santiago's quest, turns out to be unbearable.

If the newspapers cannot print "the truth," that same truth continues to circulate in the ephemeral script of spoken language. It is this script that Vargas Llosa inscribes in the body of the novel. Thus, the novel sets its truth removed from a journalistic and historical account of the period. Julio Ortega has perceptively pointed out that in *Conversation in The Cathedral,* what is orchestrated is "el habla del mal," or a sort of evil speak.[6] Queta, along with Carlitos and Santiago, becomes the practitioner par excellence of this evil speak.

On the whole, Vargas Llosa's third novel tells a sordid and scatological story at galloping rhythm. Each numbing scene is quickly followed by an even more repulsive or pornographic event. In the end the reader's feelings are permeated by a sense of fear and disgust. But such disgust is not gratuitous. On the contrary, it becomes one of the goals of the novel's story, for the reader feels motivated to repel the avalanche of fecal, viscous slimy materials and acts, as well as the moral depravity in which some of the characters become the hopeless victims of the system. The reader, like Santiago, is persuaded that it is necessary to learn more about the nature of such fetid evil in order to understand its origins, and perhaps to find an answer to Santiago's initial question: "When did Peru get all screwed up?" It is the irrevocable need to find an answer that sustains the reader's interest through the thick and thin of the novel's filth.

Almost all of the novel's characters know themselves

to be trapped and immersed in evil. The sheer, inescapable presence of evil creates a Dantesque atmosphere. Here, in this conversation, in this dingy and smelly bar where the two men sweat profusely under a cloud of hungry flies, nothing, not even love or compassion, can mitigate the feeling of dissolution that weighs down on the characters. Action does not save anyone. On the contrary, action, as in hell, merely brings on more suffering, more despair, and alienation. Everyone learns to suspect everyone else, all individuals become each other's victims. Perhaps only Amalia and La Musa live fleeting moments of happiness. Amalia is an innocent girl in a culture so foreign to her that she plainly does not understand what she sees. La Musa, whose gay, perfect smile and snow-white body are reminiscent of Marilyn Monroe, so badly wants to have a good time that she willfully closes her eyes to the treacherous intentions of her many lovers. Only the free, childish consciousness of these two exploited young women can feel and see delight where everyone else sees sexual exploitation in alliance with political abuse.

In *Conversation in The Cathedral* the factors generally assumed to forge social bonds of unity play an opposite role. In this society everything divides and alienates its members: race separates, politics divides, kinship estranges, money distances, social position isolates. Only with sex, and only for an instant, can the characters feel sufficiently free to smile or laugh. The relationship between victim and oppressor is constant, and as such it marks the rhythm of encounters and disencounters between Dante's second and seventh circles. It is as if the dogs' world in *The Time of the Hero* had spilled over to the whole of Lima. *Conversation in The Cathedral* then emerges as the most bitter and Dantesque of Vargas Llosa's novels, for Santiago's quest culminates in a dead end with no answers and no prelude to a different future.

NOTES

1. *Edges of Extremity: Some Problems of Literary Modernism* (Tulsa: University of Oklahoma Press, 1980); quoted in Gerdes, *Mario Vargas Llosa* (Boston: Twayne, 1985) 113.

2. See Jean Franco, "Conversations and Confessions: Self and Character in *The Fall* and *Conversation in The Cathedral," Texas Studies in Literature and Language* 19 (1977) 452–68.

3. Mario Vargas Llosa, *Conversación en La Catedral,* (Barcelona: Seix Barral, 1969) 2:120–21. All translations are mine; page numbers are given in parentheses.

4. José Miguel Oviedo, *Mario Vargas Llosa: La invención de una realidad,* (Barcelona: Barral Editores, 1970) 183. The translation is mine.

5. "Realismo sin limites," *Indice* 224:24; quoted in Oviedo 184.

6. See Julio Ortega, "Mario Vargas Llosa: el habla del mal," *Mario Vargas Llosa,* ed. José Miguel Oviedo (Madrid: Taurus, 1982).

CHAPTER FIVE

The Perpetual Orgy and Other Critical Writings: Self-Portrait of the Novelist

Between 1969 and 1975 Vargas Llosa published a number of articles, interviews, and books in which he attempted to explain his views on the novel as well as his own craft. His first important and influential essay was his preface to the modern edition in 1969 of the Catalonian chivalric novel *Tirant lo Blanc*. In fact, it was Vargas Llosa's earlier rediscovery of Joanot Martorell's romance that created enough interest in the nearly forgotten fifteenth-century text to warrant a modern edition in Spanish. *Tirant lo Blanc* was originally written in Catalonian and first published in Valencia in 1490. The first Spanish edition was published in Valladolid in 1511.

Although we do not know which edition Cervantes refers to in *Don Quixote*, it is clear that the master and eventual destroyer of the chivalric novel had read and liked Martorell's book. Cervantes's book-burning priest speaks in favor of saving *Tirant lo Blanc* from the flames, for he believes it to be a treasure of fun and a mine of pastimes. The priest particularly recalls the battles fought by the valiant Tirant against the Alans, Damoiselle Placerdemivida's sharp mind, Widow Reposada's love affairs and lies, and Lady Emperatriz's love for Hipólito, her squire. Above all, the priest appreciates the realistic style of the novel, because in this story "the knights eat, sleep, and die in their beds, and they make a will before their death, and they do many other things that other books of this type are lacking."[1]

At first glance it would seem curious and ironic to find Vargas Llosa's argument on behalf of the "modernity" of *Tirant lo Blanc* to be based, roughly, on the same realistic tenets of Cervantes's priest. What is even more puzzling is that Vargas Llosa never mentions Cervantes in relation to the birth of the modern novel. In Vargas Llosa's rediscovery of *Tirant lo Blanc,* the Catalonian Martorell figures as the sole precursor of the nineteenth-century French realistic novel and in particular of the art of Gustave Flaubert.

The affinity between his own work and Martorell's historical novel[2] is to be found, according to Vargas Llosa, in a mutual commitment to "capture reality on more than one plane." The author of *The Green House* calls our attention to the emphasis that Martorell places on the story, and especially on adventure as an essential quality of the novelistic plot. According to the thesis that Vargas Llosa propounds, the modern novel had its origins in this particular chivalric narrative. Furthermore, he asserts that the "chivalric novel" was repudiated by the authorities of the period because it lured man's vision away from God, thus emphasizing the flow of human affairs as a realm independent of the divine order:

> The novel, differing from other genres, is, before anything else, a proud human affirmation. Without

an essentially human problematic, there is no novel. How did the early writers of novels show the reality of their period? They showed it in an unbiased, disinterested manner. They told stories about what they saw, about what they believed in, about what they felt. Their description, their representation of the world, was, differing from what was happening in other genres, not partial, but on the contrary total, or rather, totalizing.[3]

We can see that according to Vargas Llosa's thesis, the novel, especially his own fiction, is based on the quest for a totalizing representation of what he calls "worldly matters." By making this distinction between divine and worldly matters he implicitly accepts the fifteenth-century distinction between literature written *a lo divino* and secular literature. It is once again puzzling to see that Vargas Llosa did not bring into the consideration of this distinction the long-lasting Spanish discussion about genre, verisimilitude, and textual motivation that Lope de Vega, Cervantes, and many other Golden Age authors embedded in their own *comedias,* novels, and narrative poems.

I believe that one of the reasons why Vargas Llosa consciously or unconsciously skirts the Spanish Golden Age, and even Cervantes, is that the type of hero he has in mind breaks the bounds of even Lope's and Cervantes's ample sense of verisimilitude. As we have seen earlier, Vargas Llosa's heroes, though they try, in the end find themselves unable to shake off the mask that society and life imposes upon them. More important to this point, his characters are often amoral or immoral people who never find the need or opportunity to repent or to bring together all the disconnected parts of their lives into a coherent unity. In contrast, Don Quixote engages in unbelievable adventures, but he does so because he is both mad and sane. Toward the end, however, he settles for the peaceful Christian death that comes to a good man who has recovered his sanity. In Lope's realistic plays (*comedias*) everything goes wrong. People's worst instincts and lowly desires wrack havoc in the Spain of Philip II; but in the end the Comendador de Ocaña is punished and Casilda is returned to her lawful husband. This final restoration of sanity and the status quo is most likely what renders Golden Age literature "divine" to Vargas Llosa's sensibilities and modern interests, for modern man is alienated and lost in a world that does not have neat boundaries between sin and virtue, between hell and heaven. Tirant lo Blanc, Martorell's military hero and amorous knight, appears in this sense to be more modern. Though truly conventional, he is an amoral knight.

In 1918 the first American scholar to write on *Tirant lo Blanc,* Joseph A. Vaeth, found that the romance offers enough data to surmise that Martorell was either a lawyer, a monk, or a military man. Vaeth writes that "the intensely religious spirit, sermons, and prayers, and the efforts to conquer or crush the enemies of the Holy Catholic Church point strongly in this direction."[4] He remains, however, uncertain because Martorell

> has included in his work several features that are not in harmony with a serious and lofty purpose. From these, a fair idea of his character and disposition may be obtained. He is jolly, jovial, frivolous,

> talkative, malicieux, and bold, even to the point of impertinence. He is queer and eccentric. He has peculiar ideas on the fitness of things. He shows extremely bad taste from the standpoint of the present time. Sometimes, he allows his hero to conduct himself in an undignified manner, or makes him the victim of mishaps that tend to decrease our admiration for him. And then, as a climax to these occasional disparaging portrayals, he endows his hero with a low, immoral nature.[5]

Thus, it would seem that *Tirant lo Blanc* achieves the contradictory blend and tug of high and low mimetic so characteristic of the modern fictional character. Although Vargas Llosa does not quite spell it out, it is this contradiction in the hero's makeup that inclines Vargas Llosa to see in *Tirant lo Blanc,* and not other chivalric novels, the precursor of the modern novel.

Among other points of filiation with *Tirant lo Blanc,* Vargas Llosa points out the preference for high adventure—war, siege, elopement, disguised identity, battle with bigger-than-life enemies—and for the unpredictable mixture of what he calls "verifiable reality" and "subjective reality." In a short essay, *La novela,* published in Montevideo three years before the preface to *Tirant lo Blanc,* Vargas Llosa socratically argues for the similarities between the chivalric novels and what he envisions as the modern novel or his own novels.

> What happens in chivalric novels? One tells military stories. Almost always, there are crusaders, men who go to fight in Jerusalem, adventurers who go out to combat in exotic lands, and this constitutes the objective and concrete level of reality that the [authors] incorporate in their texts. They described

> in an undoubtedly realistic fashion the weapons of their time, warfare tactics, warriors' clothing, and the rest of their war paraphernalia. In those novels, there was an immediately verifiable level of reality that the author showed.
>
> They would mix a subjective reality (Merlin the Magician or Urganda) with an objective reality, an exterior reality with a purely inner mental reality. They employed a very wide, generous concept of realism. They wanted to show reality in all its levels. . . . A novel like Joanot Martorell's is one of the books that I most admire.[6]

The coincidences between Vargas Llosa's work and the one novel written by Martorell have been long-lasting. Vargas Llosa has often returned to the subject of the chivalric novel, and particularly to this saucy, achronological, and satyrical romance. In collaboration with the Spanish man of letters Martín de Riquer, the Peruvian novelist has edited the few letters left by the unknown Martorell. In these letters Martorell challenges other knights to engage him in duel. Martorell delights in spelling out all the sartorial details and weaponry to be appointed for the ritual. Vargas Llosa is quite sensitive to Martorell's fascination with ritual, an obsession that critics have found in Vargas Llosa's own oeuvre. The author of *The Time of the Hero* writes about the fifteen *cartas de batalla:*

> We know only a few things about Joanot Martorell's life . . . and almost all of them are about duels, or rather challenges. Martín de Riquer draws from his analysis [of the letters] the figure of an ill-tempered, bellicose man of action. However, a suspicious and microscopic reading of the letters . . . reveals that,

> more profound and imperious, more elusive and discrete than love for action and killing, yet another passion feeds his texts: love for the forms of action, for the ritual that adorns the killing. This is a subtle, abstract, inoffensive, and punctilious passion.[7]

In more recent publications Vargas Llosa speaks of his initial interest in the chivalric novel as isolated from any further interest in Peninsular literature. Reminiscing about his university years both in Peru and in Spain, he points out the typically strong influence of non-Hispanic writers in Latin American intellectual life:

> I believe that my literary generation was much more influenced by other cultures than by Spain. I am speaking of the generation that attended university during the fifties.... Hispanism represented, at least in the case of Peru, something that was not very stimulating from an intellectual, political, and even moral point of view. It represented an extremely reactionary vision of history and culture.... I discovered the chivalric novel by sheer bent of contradiction. One of the professors ... said, repeating what had been written in many histories of Spanish literature, that the chivalric novel represented a very primitive, disarticulate, absurd example of the genre. [For him], some chivalric novels, apart from being formless and chaotic, could even be vile, coarse and psychaelliptic. The business of vile, coarse, and psychaelliptic spurred my curíosity.[8]

In spite of the fact that his first reading of *Tirant lo Blanc* was in Catalan during his early university years, Vargas Llosa retains a vivid recollection of this experience. He recalls that he was "immediately seduced, vampirized, cannibalized by the force of the story, the narrative strength of the book." He writes that he read it with a sense of voracity, and since then he has considered himself "addicted" to the game.[9]

Although, while in Paris during the 60s, Vargas Llosa lived in the artistic and intellectual climate in which the *nouveau roman* made its mark, he never felt caught up in the French narrative experiment. Many other Latin American writers living in France or in Latin America responded or even foreshadowed the experimental current of the French New Novel. Julio Cortázar's work is perhaps the best example of such foreshadowing of, as well as filiation with, the French aesthetics and epistemology that the *nouveau roman* embodied.

Vargas Llosa seems to have witnessed with some indifference the new novelists' attempts to write novels whose characters undermined the notion of person or personality, and whose plots undermined and denied action and adventure in social time and space. One can clearly see that the *nouveau roman* school, which questions the depth of the individual as well as his or her ability to be the subject of history or philosophy, steers in a very different direction from Vargas Llosa's love for adventure and historical mimesis. Roland Barthes has written that Robbe-Grillet's interest in the "surface of objects" makes for a writing that

> has no alibis, no resonance, no depth, keeping to the surface of things, examining without emphasis, favoring no one quality at the expense of another.... For Robbe-Grillet, the function of language is not a raid on the absolute, a violation of the abyss, but a

> progression of names over a surface, a patient unfolding that will gradually "paint" the object, caress it, and along its whole extent, deposit a patina of tentative identification, no single term of which could stand by itself in place of the presented object.[10]

From this it would seem that Robbe-Grillet's aesthetics have little in common with Vargas Llosa's functional and loaded use of the objects' names, their social and personal iconography, and above all their suggestive presence. Furthermore, differences could be established between the *nouveau roman* and Vargas Llosa's novelistic credo and practice, but this is not the place for such study. The above is simply an example that should be kept in mind in order to discriminate between the characteristics of the French New Novel and the gathering of several very different Spanish American novels under the term *nueva novela*.[11]

A closer look at Vargas Llosa's aesthetic preferences shows that many of his tastes and affinities had already been defined in Peru before his first European residence. His enthusiasm for the nineteenth-century French classics predates his early days in Paris and has survived almost intact. His articles on Gustave Flaubert, Honoré de Balzac, and Victor Hugo bear testimony to his long-lasting interest in the problem of mimesis which he calls realism. Even his passionate and conflictive readings of Camus, Sartre, and Beauvoir appear framed not only within the general question of mimesis, or what he calls "fidelity to reality," but also within the relation of fiction to history.

In his book-length study of Flaubert's aesthetics, *La orgía perpetua, Flaubert y Madame Bovary,* (1975 [*The*

Perpetual Orgy, Flaubert and Madame Bovary, 1986]), the author of *The Green House* states:

> even though almost all of them (Robbe-Grillet, Michel Butor, Claude Simon) bored me a great deal (with the exception of Beckett, who also bored me but nevertheless left me with the impression that the boredom, in his case, was justified), I always felt a certain empathy with them, because they would openly proclaim the importance of Flaubert for the modern novel.[12]

In general, Vargas Llosa's literary criticism has been determined by the particular authors that he admires. His essays on García Márquez, Flaubert, Camus, Hemingway, and Sartre are not part of a systematic or scholarly approach to either the work of the writer in question or problems in the study of Latin American, French, or American literature. What Vargas Llosa does through his criticism is, in part, to acknowledge a fruitful influence upon his own work or to recognize a determining affinity in temperament or world vision between himself and another writer. He does not base his essays on what has been written on the subject, nor does he approach other writers' work systematically or holistically. His interest is vital and personal.

And so we find that the novelist of texts full of adventures, violence, sex, and war has written not only of his joy in the adventures of the bellicose and ritualistic knight of *Tirant lo Blanc;* he has also written on the narrative technique and humor of García Márquez, Flaubert and his anguished relation to his own craft, George Bataille and his exploration of evil, the ethical commitment of Sartre and Camus, Javier Heraud's pristine poetry, and the social struggles of José María Arguedas and Sebastián Salazar Bondy in Peru. Within his prolific oeuvre as novelist, critic, and journalist Vargas Llosa has even appeared as the coauthor of books or polemical interviews such as the books edited with Oscar Collazos (*Literatura en la revolución y revolución en la literatura,* 1970) and with Angel Rama on the origins of the novel (*García Márquez y la problemática de la novela,* 1973).

A close reading of his literary criticism, in conjunction with what Vargas Llosa says of his own work in interviews such as that granted to Elena Poniatowska in *Antología Mínima de Mario Vargas Llosa* (1969), or in those collected and edited by Ricardo Cano Gaviria in *El buitre y el ave fénix: Conversaciones con Vargas Llosa* (1972), shows a pointed coincidence between Vargas Llosa's aesthetics and American New Criticism, or rather Henry James's theory of the novel. The autonomy of the fictional world, the disappearance of the auctorial voice, the use of dialogue and description, of showing rather than telling, the general ethical and emotional disengagement of the author (and even the narrator) from the acts and fate of the characters, are all postulates that James proposed in his introductions to his own novels and that Vargas Llosa shares. For Vargas Llosa, however, these postulates belong to a Flaubertian aesthetic that is in turn identified with the "modern" novel. Henry James does not appear related to this view of the novel in the texts of the author of *Conversation in The Cathedral.*

In other respects Vargas Llosa's views on the novelistic text seem to echo M. M. Bakhtin's *The Dialogic*

Imagination (1983). This is so even though Vargas Llosa does not indicate familiarity with the Soviet theoretician's work. Vargas Llosa's statement that the novel incorporates within its discourse all other genres seems to flow out of Bakhtin's essays. However, when Vargas Llosa speaks of the novel's "feeding on carcasses," "cannibalizing" all types of experiences, objects, and genres accessible to the novelist, his point of reference is Flaubert. The possible points of coincidence with Bakhtin have to be examined very cautiously, if for no other reason than because the Soviet theoretician refers to the capabilities for assimilation and regrounding (historically) demonstrated by novelistic discourse; and the Peruvian novelist, on the other hand, speaks of the individual and personal activity of a novelist like himself. Thus, for Vargas Llosa the emphasis is not on a historical process. For him the novelist is truly like a buzzard, forever in a reconnoitering flight, forever in search of the carcasses brought about by natural death or the teeth of the great hunting cats. Vargas Llosa's novelist seems less inclined to deepen into other texts and other discourses (in spite of *Aunt Julia* and *El Hablador*) than to engage in a sort of raw, unmediated experience. For instance, in considering what he calls the "real elements in *Madame Bovary*," Vargas Llosa writes that

> the degree to which the novelist is conscious of his theft varies. . . . A novel is not the product of a topic taken from life, but rather, from a conglomerate of experiences . . . that, having occurred at different times and under circumstances welled up at the bottom of the subconscious, float up gradually to the writer's imagination. Like a powerful mixing ma-

chine, the writer's imagination tears them apart, reassembles them, and thus produces a new substance that, by means of words and organization, takes on a new existence" (102).

This metaphor of the novel as a genre that feeds on the decomposition and recomposition of reality in the artist's imagination and in the writing process is easily identified with Flaubert, because the emphasis of the metaphor is on the elucidation of the process by which "reality" is turned into fiction. Outlining what he calls "Flaubert's theory of the novel," Vargas Llosa points to three key elements undeniably similar to his own views on the relation of the novel to reality. Thus, Vargas Llosa and Flaubert would contend the following: 1) "the writer employs, for his task, without any scruples, the whole of reality"; 2) the writer has a totalizing ambition; and 3) the novel must show, not judge.

In his reading of Flaubert, positing the French master as a mirror image of his own aesthetics, Vargas Llosa affirms that "the conviction that reality is merely working materials is of course obvious in Flaubert's mania for documentation.... He turns everything that happens to him into literature; his whole life is cannibalized by the novel" (103). Next to the hypothesis that the novel uses reality as working material, we find the idea that the novel is propelled by the novelist's and its own "totalizing vocation." This vision of the novel as a total representation of reality or a representation of total reality could also be ascribed to Sartre, another theoretician of the novel. But a close reading of how Vargas Llosa understands the concept of "totalization" takes us once again back to Flaubert, not to Sartre. This is because the Sartrean concept of a "totalizing novel" finds its exact meaning and context in the complicated polemics of neo-Hegelian Marxism, while Vargas Llosa's use of the term "totalization" does not seem to correspond to the complex view of history at the base of such polemics. This last point can be more fully and clearly understood by delving into Martin Jay's exhaustive book, *Marxism and Totality, The Adventures of a Concept, from Lukács to Habermas* (1984), and comparing the concept of history involved in the Marxist sense of totalization with Vargas Llosa's rather Thomistic concept of reality.

In his use of the concepts of totality and totalization Vargas Llosa once again appears to draw an analogy between the creative activity of the novelist and the representative capability of the text itself, as well as the narrative text and reality. An algebraic representation of Vargas Llosa's analogy would read thus: creator = novel = reality. Vargas Llosa refers to Flaubert's creative process as a "monstrous vocation," exposing the quirks of human misery as feeding on decomposing flesh. In repeated quotations from Flaubert's letters we begin to see the importance and meaning of the phrase "cannibal appetite." Vargas Llosa uses it to describe his own voracious, orgiastic readings of some texts, as well as the quest of his own oeuvre. Vargas Llosa's novelistic model can be called totalizing because it is cannibalistic, and inasmuch as it is a cannibalistic devouring of other human beings, it can encompass all human experience and history. He would seem to believe that one man is "the aleph" (as in Borges's "The Aleph") for all men and all times when he affirms that studying Flaubert's sources, we can witness "the entire history of mankind":

> A complete exegesis of the real [actual] materials used by Flaubert is not only impossible; it would be so extensive as to keep several generations of bloodhounds busy; once one begins to retrace the sources of a given fictional text, one discovers that each source takes us to another source, and this in turn to another, so that the totalization dovetails sooner or later with the entire history of mankind (107).

As perfect examples of this totalizing vision or vocation, Vargas Llosa offers *Madame Bovary* and *One Hundred Years of Solitude.* He has written two book-length studies on these novels, in part to understand why these texts had such an enormous impact upon him. *Madame Bovary,* he tells us, "shook the deepest strata of my being." It would appear, then, that the concept of totalization is not only descriptive or analytical, but also indicative of worth and value for Vargas Llosa. In assessing his response as reader to certain texts, his likes and dislikes, his preferences and rejections, the author considers that

> the first reason is, surely, an inclination that has caused me to prefer, ever since childhood, works built upon a rigorous and symmetrical order, works with a beginning and an end, works that close upon themselves and appear to be sovereign, self-contained. [I preferred these] over those other open-ended works, deliberately aimed at suggesting indeterminancy, vagueness, and process; things unfinished. It is possible that the latter may be more

> faithful images of reality and life—itself always unfinished, incomplete—but what I have undoubtedly looked for, in an instinctual manner, and what I have liked to find in books, movies, and paintings has not been the reflection of this infinite partiality, of this inmeasurable flow, but rather the exact opposite: totalizations, finite complexes that thanks to a bold structure, arbitrary and yet convincing, would create the illusion of synthetizing the real, of summing up life. This appetite was fully satisfied by *Madame Bovary* (18–19).

Readers less familiar with Vargas Llosa's entire critical writings are apt to limit the author's views on the writer and the novel to the content of his early essays on Sebastián Salazar Bondy and to his Caracas speech on literature as fire written in 1966. In those two essays Vargas Llosa posits literature as a "permanent insurrection" in relation to established society. Even though the Caracas speech dates from the same year as his essay on the novel, *La novela* (1966), a close reading of both texts shows a shift in Vargas Llosa's views on literature, a refinement regarding the vital processes of transformation that bond the creator to his work and a keener awareness of some categories of literary analysis. In this respect, it is once again Vargas Llosa himself who provides us with data and sources for a possible study of his intellectual biography.

In his brief book *Historia secreta de una novela* he not only documents the many sources he used for his portrayal of the jungle in *The Green House,* but also gives us a short list of what he read in order to distract himself from the anxiety involved in creating a coherent world for the disparate materials of his second novel. Among his distracting reading we find volumes of Flaubert's correspondence and almost all of Flaubert's novels. A posteriori, it is not difficult to see that he found many a solution in Flaubert's keen reflections upon his own writing as well as in *Sentimental Education, Salambó,* and *Madame Bovary.* In *Historia secreta,* Vargas Llosa continues to sustain the idea that the writer is by definition a rebel (a generalization that can always be correct); yet in the story of his search out of the impasse he met in the writing of *The Green House,* and even more clearly in *La novela,* one can detect a retreat from Sartre's committed writer, as well as the emergence of Flaubert's desire for the creation of autonomous fictional worlds.

The Sartre of *What Is Literature?* published in Spanish in 1950, had an enormous repercussion in all of Latin America. Acknowledging his debt to Sartre, Vargas Llosa has said that the author of *The Wall* saved him from *costumbrismo.*

> *Qué es la literatura* was one of the first books I read as a freshman in 1953. I went back to several of its chapters many times. At the time, I was a militant member of the Fracción Universitaria Comunista *Cahuide,* [and reread Sartre] in search of arguments for the heated discussions that we held in the group, [because] I always disagreed with my comrades on the question of culture.... During the [next] ten years, [in] all that I wrote, believed, and said on the function of literature, I glossed or plagiarized that essay [by Sartre].[13]

It is perhaps due to Vargas Llosa's public identification with *What Is Literature?* as well as the general enthusiasm for Sartre among critics and novelists that *The Time of the Hero* was originally read as an existentialist novel. It is necessary to maintain a basic distinction between the novels, critical essays, and journalism written by the same author before one can transfer, without further mediation, ideas and opinions expressed in one type of discourse to another. The "persona" who writes novels, as New Criticism definitively showed over thirty years ago when it proposed the biographical fallacy, is not the same identical "persona" of the narrative enunciation; nor does he or she turn out to be the most reliable reader of the novels bearing his or her autograph. Statements made in a journalistic context are often embedded in hyperbole; and of course fiction is fiction—otherwise fiction, biography, history, autobiography, and journalism would all blend into the same unrecognizable flow. While it is true that all these forms of discourse about the world of events bear many similarities, it is also true that the differences we have established among them continue to be all-important in our search for truth. If, furthermore, we regard Vargas Llosa's expressed criticism separately from the aesthetics embedded in his novels, it would seem that the following is true: not only the Caracas speech and the speech upon the death of the playwright Salazar Bondy, "Sebastián Salazar Bondy y la vocación del escritor en el Perú," but also "Una insurrección permanente," fall well within Sartre's concept of the writer morally committed to the historical dilemmas and ethical crises of his or her time. However, examination of other essays written by Vargas

Llosa at about the same time that he ascribes to Sartre's influence (*La novela,* "Carta de batalla por *Tirant lo Blanc*") shows that the young writer faced problems posed by new readings and new developments in the understanding of reality, especially in the political and sexual/erotic spheres. And so he searched for solutions far beyond his readings of the Sartre of *Situations, No Exit,* and *The Reprieve.* Furthermore, the Cuban revolution first, and the Herberto Padilla case later, play an important part in this reorientation of Vargas Llosa's aesthetics.

After positing writing as an act of rebellion (Sartre), Vargas Llosa seems to find himself more comfortable with Flaubert's position that writing is a sort of revenge: "For Flaubert, who repeated over his entire life that he wrote in order to take his revenge on reality, it was the negative experiences in life that he found to be artistically stimulating" (105). In the same book, while making reference to Sartre's *L'idiot de la famille,* Vargas Llosa states once more his present wide distance from Sartre and his existentialist/Marxist views on the writer's relation to literature:

> Sartre is one of the writers to whom I have a very large debt. At a certain time in my life, I admired his work almost as much as Flaubert's. With the passing of time, however, his creative work has lost its brilliance in my memory, and his postulates on literature and the function of the writer, which I once regarded as articles of faith, today seem unconvincing (541).

For Vargas Llosa, Sartre's arguments have lost their persuasive force, not only in comparison to Flaubert's modernist aesthetics, but also within the choices and contrast that the two branches of existentialism propose in the thought of Sartre and Camus. In the preface to *Entre Sartre y Camus,* a book in which Vargas Llosa brings together his essays on these two existential writers, the former admirer of Sartre summarizes the final result of his past oscillation: "I ended up embracing the literary reformism of Camus." Further, he reveals that the protracted polemics between Sartre and Camus followed a parallel course within his own thinking. After repeated reflection on the arguments and dilemmas of the two French writers, he found himself agreeing with Camus, twenty years after having sided with Sartre.

In a sort of spiritual journey Vargas Llosa chronicles the dilemma that split the ranks of the Parisian progressive intelligentsia and their Latin American followers. He recalls how the ideological differences underlying the Sartre-Camus polemic reached a climax when the existence of labor camps in the Soviet Union was made public in the West. In retrospect, he feels that the debate centered on the question of history as the sum total of the human experience or history as simply part of human destiny. Another burning issue debated was morality.

> [Does it] exist autonomously, as a reality that transcends political events and social praxis, or is it vicerally linked to historical developments and collective life[?] ... For Sartre, there was no way of escaping History ... and thus, it was necessary to support the Soviet Union, because it represented the cause of progress.... For Camus, such "realism" opened the way to political cynicism; it legitimized

> the horrible belief that the truth, within History, is determined by success.[14]

For Vargas Llosa there cannot be two kinds of terror, one positive and the other negative. For him, to refuse to choose between two kinds of injustice or barbarism is not to play the ostrich game but to revindicate for mankind a

> destiny superior to ideologies, for there is an irreducible human quality that History cannot domesticate or explain. It makes man capable of pleasure, joy, and fantasy. The reasons of History are always efficiency, action, and reason. But man is that and much more: contemplation, passion, and the irrational.[15]

Retrospectively, the author of *Conversation in The Cathedral* can see clearly that his break from Sartre is related to a reading of Sartre's political posture which appeared to deny passion, the absurd, and imagination as essential elements in the constitution of the human being. As Vargas Llosa has come to understand Sartre, in history there is no room for a dreamer in search of happiness. Sartre's theory of history, according to Vargas Llosa, would erase the vision of man's unconscious, passion, and desire.

To many a reader of the existentialist Sartre and his central concern for the absurdity of man's situation in a world without meaning, this reading of Sartre will probably prove, to say the least, surprising. To those familiar with Sartre's complex and "totalizing" concept of history, Vargas Llosa's differences with Sartre on this subject will underscore the fact that Vargas Llosa's own sense of history is decidedly non-Marxist and limiting. Perhaps Vargas Llosa's retrospective view of his present distance from Sartre places too much emphasis on the question of history and forgets Sartre's exploration of the alienated man. Still, it is noteworthy that Sartre did not envision a happy man, a joyous man, a laughing man. The entitlement to pleasure and satisfaction seems to be the wedge that drives the original filial embrace apart.

This defense of man as a passionate being entitled to satisfaction and pleasure was already present in Vargas Llosa's critical texts written long before the preface to *Entre Sartre y Camus*. In fact, it can be found already in his essays on Salazar Bondy, Oquendo de Amat, and César Moro. In these essays written in the late 60s the image of the writer as rebel emerges unambiguously. However, where many readers saw only a political rebel, Vargas Llosa probably meant a rebel on all fronts, especially a rebel against conventional morality, a morality of restrictions, privations, and denial of desire. Vargas Llosa seems to rebel against Catholic social mores, and especially against the catechismal notion of sin. He reserved for the writer a noncontingent freedom which guaranteed him the right to rebel against any and all limitations in the name of creativity. A number of postulates on man's freedom to dream and desire, and above all on the artist as an irrationally free (but possessed) being, inform his *García Márquez, historia de un deicidio* (1971).[16]

The scholarship that took him in the late 50s to study literature in Spain came to fruition some ten years later in a doctoral dissertation on García Márquez's narrative technique. Vargas Llosa develops the thesis that the novelist is a man inhabited by demons, possessed by powerful obsessions. The struggle to expel the demonic creatures constitutes the source of the novelist's world and will to write. This Freudian image holds that the demons and obsessions forged by the personal experiences of the writer unaware of the dynamics of his inner self dictate his choices of topic, combination of themes, problems, and solutions found in his narrative text. Vargas Llosa develops this thesis by bringing together data from García Márquez's life and information derived from *One Hundred Years of Solitude* as well as the short stories of the Colombian master. In carrying out this "life and works" type of study Vargas Llosa uses the same type of literary analysis that he employed in the self-examination of his own creative work. This can be easily documented in the background interviews he has given before or after the publication of each of his major novels. *Historia secreta de una novela* is the most accessible example. In this context it would appear that the problematics displayed in the course of the novelistic discourse is directly autobiographical, because the composition of the texts is squarely framed within the parameters of Freud's theory of repression. According to this theory the conscious unsuccessfully attempts to repress the subconscious part of the psyche.

When he proposes this thesis in his book on García Márquez, just as he later does in his essays on Flaubert, Vargas Llosa carefully looks for homological relations between the materials in the text and the emotional, physical, or intellectual experiences of the author. This type of reading of a fictional text would seem to contradict another of Vargas Llosa's postulates, namely the total autonomy of a fictional text from its creator as individual or historical being. If the text is a weaving of the life experiences and obsessions of its author, who in addition to being a man gifted with a rich subconscious is accosted by the demands and censorship of his ego (the internalization of social and historical structures), we find that Vargas Llosa's thesis has not led him that far from Sartre's original formulation of the writer's relation to society. The irony in Vargas Llosa's position is especially underlined by the fact that, in *L'idiot de la famille,* Sartre proposes the crossroads for a literary analysis in which both Freudian and neo-Marxist categories are brought together in order to produce a deeper and more complete understanding of Flaubert as author of a particular world view.

In the book on García Márquez the greater part of the biographical material seems to come from the Colombian author himself. At the time both writers were close friends, and García Márquez seems to have volunteered an autobiographical sketch for Vargas Llosa's book. In *The Perpetual Orgy* the biographical information used by Vargas Llosa seems to have its main source in the thirteen volumes of Flaubert's published correspondence. In both cases Vargas Llosa relies on the author's self-portrayal of his life and work. Even though there is a remarkable difference between private correspondence and conversation with a friend as sources for biographical studies, both sources seem to enjoy the status of authorized autobiographies in Vargas Llosa's mind.

It is interesting to note how in his book on Flaubert, Vargas Llosa returns to the same critical terminology and concepts that he had proposed almost ten years earlier in his book on García Márquez. For Vargas

Llosa 1) the novel is a "totalizing" text; 2) its narrative rhetoric is made up of "mutations" in the narrator; 3) the narrative presents a created world that emerges as a result of the combination of several planes of reality as well as diverse temporal lines. These characteristics of fiction, together with the hypothesis that modern novelists (the "true heirs to Flaubert") erect themselves in their own texts as a sort of God, have their origins in Flaubert's own aesthetics. *The Perpetual Orgy* proves an excellent text for the documentation of Flaubert's influence on Vargas Llosa's aesthetics. There he writes that "each novelist creates the world in his own image. He corrects reality in relation to his own demons. What is subjective material in Flaubert, in fictional reality becomes an objective fact" (148).

Reflecting on Flaubert's play with the time of the enunciation, the time of the action, historical time, and the *durée* within a character's consciousness, Vargas Llosa speaks of the temporal planes in *Madame Bovary:*

> The four temporal planes that I have made reference to establish a division among the historical data that is not marked by durability but, rather, by substance. And the mutations of the narrator, shifting the story from one plane to another, owe their complexity to the fictional world. . . . The narrator covers up these changes, the reader is barely conscious of the continuous rotation of the narrative materials (153).

Referring to one of his own most distinguishing and widely used narrative techniques, shifts in the enunciation, Vargas Llosa finds it to be crucial in the seemingly unmediated telling of Emma's story. He points out how important are "[the] mutations of the narrator who actually tells the story of Madame Bovary." Vargas Llosa still revels in the idea that Flaubert used "several narrators whose voices are revealed with such subtlety that the reader hardly notices the changes in point of view, and thus is left with the impression that the narrator is actually a single voice" (123).

Vargas Llosa not only deploys these concepts for the analysis of works in which he finds a remarkable affinity with his own writings, but he has also used them in interviews and essays to explain diverse aspects of his own novelistic praxis and goals. He seems particularly interested in the idea of transforming the author into an invisible presence in the novelistic text. The author is thus analogous to the Christian God. He/God appears as a contradictory creator inasmuch as he is the author of his creation but remains inaccessible for the duration and meaning of his creation. God's own plan and understanding is denied to the consciousness and senses of his creatures. In Vargas Llosa's argument, the author's creatures are not the characters but rather the readers, those readers who fall into the trap of believing that the narrator is a single voice. However, upon closer examination this Godlike author seems more reminiscent of Borges's demiurges than of the more logical God of Christian theology. Like Borges's mad demiurges, this author/God not only plays at not being present in the world of his creation, but also disclaims responsibility for his creation. It would seem that for Vargas Llosa, for the novelistic world to be modern, it must appear to beguiled readers as a sovereign and autonomous world.

In the texts of those writers with whom he finds a temperamental or aesthetic affinity, Vargas Llosa finds shared attitudes towards sex, sexuality, genre, and the will to write. It would not be an exaggeration to suggest that the author of *The Time of the Hero* began to write under the alienating gaze of his father's censorship. The writer has often said that his father regarded writers as failed or strange, weird men. The father's negative and disapproving attitude seems to be embodied by the social reality and the public persona of the poet César Moro, who is in fact, and according to Vargas Llosa himself, the historical referent for the professor of French in *The Time of the Hero*. The writer posited by Vargas Llosa's view of the author has to evaluate his desire to write and the pleasure of writing, within the context of the father's dire predictions and prohibition. The figure and destiny of César Moro—a brilliant but obscure surrealist poet, a Peruvian who wrote in French, a secret homosexual—seems to throbe in the father's warnings and denials. The image of the marginal writer—the object of his contemporaries' scorn and satire—activates Vargas Llosa's view of the writer as a perpetual rebel, as a challenger to the status quo, as the man who points the finger at the hypocrisy of the social code. The writer as rebel would seem to be the reply to the father's image of the writer as failure. It is in this vein that Vargas Llosa finds his solidarity with the person and work of Sebastián Salazar Bondy, a feeling that he made very plain the night he received the Rómulo Gallegos Prize in Caracas.

Apparently César Moro felt that he engaged in two secretive and forbidden activities: writing poetry and homosexual desire. Although he kept them to himself, he acknowledged the nature of his desire and his acts by lending poetry and pornographic or erotic books to those seemingly interested in his secret realm. Vargas Llosa's association with this *poet maudit* seems to have left in him the notion that writing is an act of transgression. Such transgression may be totally involuntary, without a particular cause or purpose; but it is in any case a forbidden act, an act against what has been established, perhaps, by the writing of previous generations. Because in Latin America writing, the law, and power were until recently the monopoly of the state and the groups it represented, it is easy to see how Vargas Llosa moves from linking writing with transgression to associating writing with revenge and exorcism. Thus he says that

> literature is an attempt to recover the past, as a way of exorcising a set of given passions. When one writes, one tries to free oneself from something that, in a rather obscure way, is the cause of anxiety. One tries to rescue, to relive, to save from the pit of oblivion a certain type of experiences that have marked one's person profoundly, but that somehow one is not yet ready to let die.[17]

NOTES

1. Miguel de Cervantes, *El ingenioso hidalgo Don Quixote de la Mancha,* ed. and annotated by Francisco Rodríquez Marín, 2 vols. (Madrid, 1911) 1:160–63. The translation is mine.

2. For a careful portrayal of *Tirant lo Blanc* as a novel based on the lives of the historical Roger de Flor, Guy of Warwick, Richard of Beauchamp, Peter the Second of Aragon, and other military heroes

of the period, see Joseph A. Vaeth, *Tirant lo Blanc, a Study of Its Authorship, Principal Sources, and Historical Setting* (New York: Columbia University Press, 1918) esp. 159.

3. Mario Vargas Llosa, *La novela,* (Montevideo, 1966) 15–16 passim. All translations are mine.

4. Vaeth 160.

5. Vaeth 169–70.

6. *La novela* 17.

7. Martín de Riquer and Mario Vargas Llosa, *El combate imaginario: Las cartas de batalla de Joanot Martorell,* (Barcelona: Barral, 1972) 9.

8. Mario Vargas Llosa, "La experiencia de los novelistas," interview with José Miguel Oviedo *Revista Iberoamericana* 48 (1981) 317.

9. "La experiencia de los novelistas," 318.

10. Roland Barthes, "Objective Literature: Alain Robbe-Grillet," *Two Novels by Robbe-Grillet,* trans. Richard Howard (New York: Grove Press, 1965) 12.

11. Carlos Fuentes's *La Nueva Novela hispanoamericana,* (México: Joaquín Mortiz, 1969), could lend itself to such confusion.

12. Mario Vargas Llosa, *La orgía perpetua, Flaubert y Madame Bovary* (Barcelona: Seix Barral, 1975) 49. All translations are mine; page numbers are given in parentheses.

13. Mario Vargas Llosa, *Entre Sartre y Camus,* (Río Piedras: Huracán, 1981) 109.

14. *Entre Sartre y Camus* 12–13.

15. *Entre Sartre y Camus* 12–13.

16. For an indepth discussion of the irrational thesis in Vargas Llosa's concept of the writer, see the polemic with Angel Rama in *García Márquez y la problemática de la novela,* (Buenos Aires: Corregidor/Marcha, 1973).

17. "Conversación con Vargas Llosa," *Imagen* 6 (1967) 5.

CHAPTER SIX

The Realm of Parody: Pantaleón and Aunt Julia

At times it seems as though Vargas Llosa's critical appraisal of other writers' work were an emblematic manner of opening his own creative enterprise to other possibilities. After the book on García Márquez's literary technique and humor, and especially after the self-revealing book on Flaubert, Vargas Llosa published his first satirical novel, *Pantaleón y las visitadoras* (1973 [*Captain Pantoja and the Special Service,* 1978]). In this text Vargas Llosa makes ample use of the conventions of parody. He also goes back to many of the themes and social concerns of his earlier work. Once again the plot weaves multiple threads: 1) the blind hierarchical organization of the military; 2) the dominant presence and dynamics of sexual exchange, either within the family structure or at the brothel; and 3) the unraveling of civilization and the return to the primeval in the context of the Peruvian jungle.

The scatological character of the reality represented in *Captain Pantoja and the Special Service* is blown up in the logic of the plot and in the scenes of this novel. However, a relentless humor, largely based on the cartoon technique of exaggeration, colors and transforms the tragedy lived by the characters into a farce enjoyed by the reader. Pantaleón's efforts to succeed in his job—to organize a service of prostitutes available to the army garrisons posted in the jungle. In general, the humor employed is crude, relying as it does on the social stereotypes and sexual myths of a *machista* culture. The novel's humor is based on exaggeration of numbers, size, feelings, and gender, as well as on the transgression of social codes based on a hierarchical social organization. Above all, the laughter provoked by Pantaleón appeals to the coding of the *huachafo* and the upper-class put-down of the provincial and the half-educated.[1]

Pantaleón is a military officer who, like Gamboa in *The Time of the Hero,* takes the military and its myths about itself very seriously. Unlike Gamboa, however, Pantaleón is, above all, a *cholito.*[2] He is not quite attuned to the underside of *criollos'* sense of humor; he does not exactly get the double entendre of the social situation or the speech context. Pantaleón the *cholito* does not understand the body language that subverts the verbal statement. The *cholito* believes that a wink is truly a dysfunction in the muscles of the superior's eyelid. *Cholos* like Pantaleón believe in the systems described by *criollos;* they are unable to understand that the system of rules is merely a ruse set up to make sure that the *cholitos* carry on with their assigned role in life: to serve and further the interest of *criollos* or masters. Pantaleón is a lucky *cholito,* for he has not only managed entrance into the military service but has actually been promoted on the basis of his own merits. Knowing himself to be a lucky *cholito,* he obeys dutifully, studies to improve his performance, and marries a joyful little *cholita.* Pochita, his wife, someday might even become a *criolla.* Somewhere in

Pantaleón's mind there is a little light that lets him know that he is actually mediocre and that no matter how hard he tries, he will never really catch on to the subtleties of *criollos*. He is a good *zonzo* (sardine) surrounded by *vivos* (sharks). Obedience and efficiency have not only saved him so far but have carried him a long way—all the way to captain. But his new assignment in the jungle will more than test his military organizational expertise. It will test his judgment. The plot in *Captain Pantoja* revolves around the following questions: Will Pantaleón, like Napoleon, succumb in a foreign land? Will he be able to improvise? Will he tinker successfully with systems devised elsewhere, so as to produce a *criollo* solution to the army's sexual problems?

If Pantaleón had been more of a *criollo,* if he had come from a slightly higher social class to begin with, he would have contrived not to accept his assignment. He would have suspected that the whole idea of providing safe and adequate sexual satisfaction for the army troops based in the Amazon jungle was by definition an impossible task. But Panta-león, the lion without pants, the insufficiently *macho* officer, the officer previously in charge of the laundry, the kitchen, and the clothing of his barracks, does not question his officers. He, like many others in society, particularly women, has been trained to receive orders. If, in obeying, he will make an ass of himself, it won't matter, for he has also been trained to bear humiliation at the hands of his superiors. In the end Pantaleón will exceed the limits of the obedient "inferior" officer to join the general ranks of the *huachafo,* the person who imitates his or her own model without question. Such servile and uncritical imitation of the object of admiration on the part of the *huachafo* informs much of the satire and parody in this novel.

Some critics have seen in this modern parody more than a tinge of the grotesque.[3] As in *Aunt Julia and the Scriptwriter* the grotesque appears here in connection with the lives of the *lumpen,* the groveling masses. Such *lumpen* can be urban, as in the world that Camacho conjures up in his radio soap operas; or it can be rural, such as the people involved in the cult of the Brotherhood of the Arch in *Captain Pantoja,* or the counselor's followers in *The War of the End of the World.* In Vargas Llosa's parodial novel, the grotesque appears as an asymmetrical madness to Pantoja's own derangement. In the excesses of the Brotherhood of the Arch we find an unleashing of the sadistic and satanic fantasies that not even Cayo Bermúdez would have contemplated. The Arch's macabre infanticide, crucifixions, blood-drinking, and sexual excesses provide an unbridled version of the statistically contained administration of sexual pleasures and exploitation devised by Pantaleón. Religious fervor is assumed to be the cause and justification for the horrifying crimes committed by the Brotherhood while a maniacal, consumerist, statistical rage seems to be the cause for the services that Pantaleón provides. The pornographic crucifixion of mammals and insects, the head-bashing of children, the mortification of the flesh, and the sexual orgies of the cult encompass the mise-en-scène of some of the most grotesque fantasies of violence and sex in Latin American literature.

Discourse Parody and the Plot

Captain Pantoja's story is told by means of a most diverse and creative use of modern narrative rhetoric and by the parodial imitation of journalistic and bureaucratic discourses. In an unspoken challenge to his own previous dazzling use of narrative technique, Vargas Llosa creates a new narrative modality in which he does away almost completely with the presence of a narrator in charge of the totality of narrative materials and sources of the story. *Captain Pantoja* emerges out of the materials and relations established in and within different documents and types of discourse. Dialogues, letters, maps, radio commentary, print media articles, official memoranda, scientific charts and articles, interior monologue, and rumor constitute the fragments of discourse brought together in the book as vehicles that tell Pantaleón's story.

Pantaleón's story, like the stories of many of Vargas Llosa's characters, is brief but thickened by high adventure. It would seem that this simple man's modest desires reach their culmination in his marriage with Pochita and his promotion to captain. His satisfaction even includes his mother-in-law, who joins the happy couple in expectation of the birth of their first child. Everything changes with his posting to Iquitos and his new, secret assignment. Based on his previous record in the procurement of food, clothing, and shoes for the army, Pantaleón's military superiors select him as the ideal man for the procurement of another domestic function: sex for the satisfaction of male appetite. He must procure adequate sex for the troops stationed in the Peruvian Amazon Basin. While procuring food and clothes is recognized by his superiors to be a publicly accepted occupation for a military man, the procurement of sex is not. He is instructed to dress and behave like a civilian. Pantaleón should know that this provision already contains the seeds of his eventual fall, but he gladly resolves to apply his well-known organizational skills to the problem.

Everything goes according to plan. He calculates exactly the number of orgasms that his consumers need, and sets out to hire enough prostitutes to supply his demand. He and his convoy punctually arrive by hydroplane or boat, render precisely timed services, and depart. But his love of precision and pride in the quality of his product bring about his misfortune. After months of arriving on time with his convoy of prostitutes, supervising the timing of each exchange, and ensuring the troops' satisfaction, on the boat back to his headquarters in Iquitos he notices that his merchandise is sitting idle. He decides to have a taste himself. As in a commercial advertisement in which the producer consumes his own product to persuade his prospective purchaser of how good it is, Pantaleón tries sex with the supreme whore, the Brazilian. He is hooked forever.

His indefatigable diligence makes him feel the obligation to continue with the service, even though it is clear that his tastes have gone beyond a mere sampling. The captain falls prey to the Brazilian's aphrodisiac. He begins to feel possessive of her. She gets more rest and more pay. He arranges to have better and more private quarters for her—and himself. He starts spending less time at home.

The word leaks out about the nature of the service

and the changed nature of his management. Pochita hears disquieting rumors. The villagers near the bases make it known that they feel that they too should benefit from the government's services. Pantaleón is confused by the conflict within him, although he seems oblivious to the turmoil that his services are creating in the society around him.

Almost at the end of the story, when Pantaleón begins to realize that his consumptive relationship with the Brazilian, as well as his home life, are threatened, the news begins to arrive in Iquitos about the infanticidal cult. The final blow to Pantaleón's mathematically calculated operation comes from the radio newscaster Sinchi. The commentary of the warrior (Sinchi means "warrior" in Quechua) contains and arouses the same irrationality that the Brotherhood of the Arch and the outraged middle-class morality of Iquitos express. Envious of Pantaleón's possessions and products, Sinchi denounces the immorality of the service, the high wages paid to the prostitutes, and the inequality created between the Peruvian military and civilians. The hypocritical military high command, which at first pretends to know nothing about Pantaleón or his services, denounces the whole idea, rescinds Pantaleón's mission, demotes him, and posts him to the end of the world, a station in the high Andes. Thus, after having failed in the military and in *criollo* society, Pantaleón is exiled, like Lieutenant Gamboa in *The Time of the Hero,* to Puno, the *criollos'* social and political equivalent of Siberia.

Parody and Discourse

There can be no doubt that in this novel Vargas Llosa essays a new departure in his narrative. The satirical tone is completely new and even surprising in light of his previous work. The narrative technique bent on creating the illusion of unmediated incorporation of documentary and empirical forms of discourse is yet another step in Vargas Llosa's exploration of realism. Mimesis here engages the image or the sensory perception of the real, but it also reproduces one of its most abstract symbolic systems: writing itself. The novel not only imitates life, but it also imitates the discourse of documents otherwise taken to be one with life itself. The letter, the memorandum, the news bulletin, as instances of a verbal symbolic order, appear almost unaware of the fact that they too are writing, that is, fabrication. Inasmuch as they are a fabrication, they share more with the craft of fiction than with some unassailable truth identical with the raw happenings of events.

Because of the new light tone, in contrast or in combination with the empirical status of the documentary discourses used as vehicles of the narrative, many critics were puzzled and confused by *Captain Pantoja and the Special Service*. Some critics wondered if the Peruvian novelist, at the height of his success, had abandoned his earlier convictions regarding the critical and subversive nature of literature. Was literature still fire? Was the writer still a committed writer? Other critics argued that *Captain Pantoja,* even though a comic novel inasmuch as it was parody, sustained a sharp critique of the status quo and of the hypocrisy upon which society is based. According to this interpretation Vargas Llosa remains faithful to his notion that literature is a constant insurrection against the established norms of perception, against all kinds of a priori assumptions.

However, the motifs in *Captain Pantoja* do not really depart from Vargas Llosa's earlier themes. In *Captain Pantoja,* as in *The Time of the Hero, Conversation in The Cathedral,* and *The Green House,* we find once again the pseudohero (Alberto, Jaguar, Santiago/Zavalita, Fushía, Lituma); the barracks, the military as a system of social organization and perception, the brothel, and the supreme prostitutes (Golden Toes, La Musa, Queta, la Selvática, the Brazilian); marriage and the family; the religious sect or the pact (The Circle, the Champs, the Brotherhood of the Arch, the Cahuide group); and the jungle.

It may seem that religious fanaticism appears here for the first time; yet this is in fact an issue that Vargas Llosa had begun to explore in his earlier novels. The common denominator is, not the religious aspect, but rather the blind acceptance and following of a leader's orders. In *The Time of the Hero* we witness the boys' acceptance and execution of Jaguar's orders to commit crimes that violate the physical, psychological, and sexual integrity of those perceived as "other." Jaguar's circle is depicted in opposition to the army's organization, which demands obedient compliance with orders no matter what their content might be. In *The Green House* the group pact is once again examined in the dynamics of the Champs and their victory over Lituma's reluctance to see his wife prostituted. The examination of the relation between ideology and fanaticism will emerge full-blown in *The War of the End of the World* and *The Real Life of Alejandro Mayta,* while its counterface of doubt and questioning had already been portrayed in Santiago's agonizing dilemmas.

Of course, *Captain Pantoja* is most easily associated wit *The Green House* in that both stories are set in the jungle. A third but rather different jungle book has come to join these two novels. In it, the military and religious orders play at "civilizing" the Aguarunas, the Huambisas, the Shapras, and many other Amazonian peoples. *El Hablador* (1987 [*The Storyteller,* 1989]) completes the Amazonian triptych, making the questioning of the white man's or his surrogate's burden more explicit. In *Captain Pantoja,* Vargas Llosa attempts to orchestrate the many written forms of *criollo* discourse in their experience of the jungle and the societies that they are creating there. In *El hablador* he pits the discourse of an anthropologist who questions his own relation to the people he studies against the discourse of a Machiguenga storyteller and Vargas Llosa's own autobiographical discourse on his discovery of the Peruvian jungle. The fascination of the author of *The Green House* with the Peruvian jungle seems a sustained inquiry into the story materials that assault his consciousness every time he visits the vast uncharted expanse of Peruvian territory. While in *The Green House,* Jum's story plays a sort of supporting role, in *El hablador* the myth of origins related by the Machiguenga wise man comes to occupy the forefront of the novel's story and discourse. In each instance the jungle materials have taken a different course within the dynamics of the writer's imagination, moving from the scatological scenes of *The Green House* through the grotesque and parodial tenor of *Captain Pantoja,* to the almost lyrical myth of origins and sense of good in *El hablador*.

Vargas Llosa has freely discussed the origin of his jungle materials. As in the case of *The Green House,* Pantaleón's story seems to be part of recent Amazonian oral history. In an interview with Ricardo Cano Gaviria the author tells how he heard people around Iquitos discussing the story of the visiting prostitutes:

> It's a very funny story. The first time we went through a series of small towns, and always, when we talked to the local folks, everywhere, they complained about the soldiers in the border garrisons. The townspeople complained about how the soldiers on their weekend pass would get drunk and rape the local women. In order to solve the problem, a service was installed: The Special Visiting Service. I don't know if it still exists. A sort of flying brigade would depart from the main towns. It would visit periodically all the garrisons. . . . Well, dating from that initial trip, I kept notes, I was planning on writing the story, but rather, the story of the officer or officers whom the Army entrusted with the Service. . . . I found it very stimulating to imagine the things he found himself forced to do. . . . This is my first light-hearted text. As you said earlier, I have a good many reservations about humor in literature. . . . I think it's a very dangerous element.[4]

To summarize, we find in Captain Pantoja an open, extraordinary, and novel representation of the *huachafo*. By such a Peruvianism we understand the linguistic habits, clothing styles, aspirations, social codes, desires, and self-conception characteristic of certain layers of Peruvian, or even Latin American, society caught between a higher layer that *huachafos* admire and emulate, and a lower layer that *huachafos* fear and despise as the image they hope to banish from their own reality. Pochita's very name, an imitation of the non-Hispanic diminutives used by the urban upper classes for females in their families, and the sentimental, false, and decorous sensitivity of her letter-writing style are excellent renditions of the *huachafo*. The *huachafo* is a bit comparable to Dolly Parton's or Cher's "elegance" before the stars won the day and their clothing style became emblematic of a certain type of celebrity. The falsely moralistic self-righteousness, and pretentious vocabulary of Sinchi's newscasting is a good example of the mindless imitation that the *huachafo* incarnates. The pompous language and empty content of the army's communiques, in which certain phrases are ritualistically employed, serve as another example of the *huachafo*. The *huachafo* is a parody—though an unconscious and unintended one—of the much desired model. *Captain Pantoja* is therefore both an imitation and a parody of the *huachafo* social and linguistic formation rampant in the hierarchical structure of Peruvian society. Within such a hierarchy of models and desires, anyone or anything can be regarded at any given moment as *huachafo* by those who establish the norms at the top. One day high-heel boots constitute the latest fashion; the next day boots are out in the hot jungle and tennis shoes are in, in accordance with the model set by a distant, unattainable authority. The *huachafo* is constantly destabilized by the norm; he agonizes between a *not being* of his own and the desire to be a reflection of his model.

Just as in previous novels, Vargas Llosa finds in *Captain Pantoja* a rich set of possibilities in which to register the repertoire of the *huachafo* within the realm of high-brow literature. In both *Captain Pantoja* and *Aunt Julia* he proposes a new problem for Latin American literature: How can a literary text considered canonical (that is, belonging to the category of great books) be a parody of noncanonical and nonliterary discourse? There remain many problems for further consideration in the assessment of a parodial literature that for the first time masters a type of humor that can be decoded at the local, national, and international levels. It is important to remember that humor has not generally traveled well, for humor seems to be one of the most locally bound symbolic orders. *Don Quixote,* for instance, is just not as funny in English as it has remained in Spanish. Perhaps the answer lies in the ideology that informs the humor.

Another problem that *Captain Pantoja,* like *Aunt Julia,* poses for its readers is the fact that in spite of its brilliant poly-glossia, its deft parody of fragments of other nonfictional discourses, the novel itself is the writing of a single consciousness; it is this consciousness that lends the various fragments the coherence of a single, unified text. This problem of unity of meaning and structure will become even more challenging in the interpolated presentation of the story (stories) of *Aunt Julia and the Scriptwriter.*

Aunt Julia and the Multiplicity of Autobiography

In *Captain Pantoja* the narrative text presents the smooth illusion of objectivity in the mix of an almost absent master narrator with the self-evidence of documentary materials. In *Aunt Julia and the Scriptwriter,* however, Vargas Llosa experiments with the exact opposite set of problems. This novel not only purports to be the autobiography of Marito (the written self), as seen and recollected by Mario Vargas Llosa (the writing self), but it also deploys another full-fledged narrator: Pedro Camacho. This second narrator is in charge of a set of fictional narratives that take place at the same time that Marito is learning his writing craft from Camacho and, in the process, passes from adolescence to manhood. Through its emphasis on writing and its focus on two narrators who write that they write, *Aunt Julia* shatters the mirror of objective mimesis into fragments of plots, failed writing attempts, and the discontinuity of writing itself.

Aunt Julia intertwines two threads previously explored by Vargas Llosa: autobiography in *The Time of the Hero* and *Conversation in The Cathedral,* and parody in *Captain Pantoja and the Special Service.* This time, within the parameters of the autobiographical pact in which the author's name is the same as the lead character's name, Vargas Llosa tells the story of Marito and his passion for his aunt Julia. The historical period evoked is once again Lima during the late 1950s. Marito is at the time enrolled as a law student at San Marcos University. He lives in Miraflores in the house of his maternal grandparents, but the entire Llosa family enjoys a sort of tribal relation in which aunts, uncles, and cousins see a lot of each other. The adolescent Marito works at the Panamericana Radio Station recasting bits of information from the print media into broadcast news bulletins. His greatest headache is to control his assistant, Pascual, who has a penchant for catastrophic, apocalyptic events.

This routine set-up in the life of the college student is disturbed by the arrival of a Bolivian relative of the Llosa family. Aunt Julia has come to live with her sister and brother-in-law while recovering from her recent divorce in Bolivia. The family hopes that, even though she is divorced, her charming personality and good looks might win her a good husband in Peru. Since Aunt Julia has no friends in Lima, the young man is encouraged to escort his aunt to the movies. In general the family expects its scion to provide entertainment for his aunt so that she may more easily forget her recent sadness. One thing leads to another, and Marito falls madly in love with Julia. She responds to his seduction, reluctantly at first, and passionately later on. Marito's own desire becomes overwhelming. He refuses to be addressed by his family nickname, grows a moustache, and proposes marriage to Aunt Julia. After this, in recognition of his manhood, she calls him Varguitas. She uses the father's last name to acknowledge his sexual manhood, but at the same time the diminutive attached to it signals Marito's continuing economic and social dependence on others. In spite of the family's unyielding opposition, his father's death threats and challenges to a public duel, the couple elope. In one of the desert towns south of Lima they manage to find a phony mayor willing to be bribed and able to sign their marriage license.

The Alternating Flow of Mock Autobiography and Parody

This story of romantic and incestuous passion is narrated in eleven chapters that alternate with Pedro Camacho's soap-opera episodes. Pedro Camacho, coincidentally, is Bolivian. Like Pascual, he is obsessed by the scatological and the apocalyptic. Camacho works for the same family of media magnates that Marito does but writes his soap operas for Radio Central, a station that caters to the less sophisticated but ever-growing urban masses. Camacho's stories of incest, bloody crime, betrayal, and changed identity capture the imagination of the entire population of Lima. Marito's aunts, and even Julia, live glued to the afternoon broadcasts of Camacho's cliffhangers. The radio soap operas now take the time formerly reserved for the siesta. In the evening Marito returns from his jaunts at the university, the cafe life of downtown Lima, and his newscasting. To get the results of Camacho's latest murder, rape, infanticide, arson, or flood, he makes a beeline for the sitting room of his aunts.

Camacho's public is unaware, however, of how hard the scribbler toils to keep up with the demands for new episodes for his several ongoing soaps. Marito, awed by Camacho's rate of production, befriends his colleague, hoping to learn the secrets of fiction writing from his visits to the Bolivian's rat-infested apartment. While Marito tries to write short stories based on anecdotes, attempting but failing to convert the flow of oral narrative into literature, Aunt Julia points out to him that their own love affair belongs in Camacho's fictional world. But Marito, who has different ideas about his writing aspirations, dismisses Aunt Julia's comments, forbids her to read her favorite sentimental novels, and tells her that she is simply a *huachafa* when it comes to literary matters:

> We used to play the game of professor and student. I would explain to her what *huachafo* was, what could not be said or be done. I had established an inquisitorial censorship over her readings. I forbade her favorite writers, Frank Yerby and Corín Tellado. We had great fun. Sometimes, Javier would intervene, with a fiery dialectic, in the *huachafería* game.[5]

Even though Camacho is characterized as a writing machine, Marito, who deeply admires Camacho's dextrous management of nine simultaneous plots, believes that the Bolivian must be following some invisible master code. In his own failed attempts to write fiction, he seems unable to locate that master code. He tears up his own unsatisfactory stories, one after the other. For the moment his only writing skill seems limited to the ability to cut and paste from other texts, thus reproducing for radio broadcasting what the print media has devised as "news." It is easy to see that, in form and content, the entire book is structured around the question of the production of texts and of their imitation and parody of themselves. In a manner reminiscent of Borges's "The Circular Ruins," what *Aunt Julia* deals with is the attempt to produce a copy of the copy, in the hope that by some unexpected quirk the scribbler might be able to manipulate the hidden secrets of a master code and produce the illusion of originality.

Trying to explain his affection and admiration for the strange, hobbling little scribbler, the young journalist argues that Camacho is the only full-time fiction writer who manages to live from what he writes, and lives in order to write. But Marito is not unaware that the fiction that Camacho writes for his radio soap operas is not really literature, no matter how popular his incestuous and sacrilegious plots may be. The aspiring writer indicts all lawyers, novelists, and playwrights who have written only a small number of poems and novels, spend most of their time at their real jobs, and unlike Camacho, see in literature a sort of secondary, ornamental occupation. In an impassioned defense of Camacho, Marito rhetorically asks his reader:

> Why should those pompous characters who used literature as ornament or pretext be considered writers more genuine than Camacho, a man who lived exclusively to write? Because they had read (or at least they knew that they should have read) Proust, Faulkner, and Joyce, and Pedro Camacho was nearly illiterate? Whenever I thought about such things, I felt sad and anxious. Every day, I realized that the only thing I wanted to be was to be a writer, and every time, I also saw that the only way to become a writer was to give my body and soul to literature. I did not want to be a half-time writer, a writer by little bits, but rather, a true writer; but like whom? The closest thing to a full-time writer obsessed and impassioned by his vocation that I had come across, anyway, was the Bolivian writer of soap operas: this is why it bothered me so much (235–36).

Marito's model is indeed troublesome. It shows a way, a total commitment to one's desire to write, but it also questions the nature of "literature."

In a parody of what we have come to identify as Vargas Llosa's own novelistic themes and techniques, the Bolivian begins to transfer characters, events, and plot lines from one story into another. At the point of paroxysm in his nine ongoing plots Camacho resurrects characters, shifts their identity radically, transfers them from one type of action to another, and even uses characters from Vargas Llosa's previous novels. Marito alerts the owners of Radio Central. He believes that such freedom can be dangerous. But the owners of the radio station can think only about ratings; they think that Camacho's mimetic transgressions are in fact the mark of genius. Only a genius could blend all the nine separate plots into one single whirlwind of action.

In the end, as Marito forewarned, the Bolivian, like a Borgesian monster, loses his mind. Camacho loses track of his metamorphosed characters and intertwined plot lines, and brings about the final solution by visiting catastrophic endings on his fictional worlds. In spite of his protest to the effect that it is not he who mixes up the characters, but the characters themselves who mutate and metamorphose, the plots of his nine stories end in an impossible tangle. For their part his radio listeners are ready to forgive him any excess for the sake of excitement and scandal, but they cannot ultimately bear his final transgression: radical changes of identity and resurrection of dead characters.

When final and total chaos rains down on Camacho's

fictional world, the owners of Radio Central, following public demand, cancel his show and call on Marito to take over. Accustomed as he is to write and rewrite bits of news until they can stand on their own as fragments of reality, Marito agrees to attempt the assemblage of the broken puzzle left behind by the scribbler. Even though the story of *Aunt Julia and the Scriptwriter* ends ambiguously, the final vision left with the reader is a scene in which Marito, now Mario Vargas Llosa, returns triumphantly to Lima from Europe. The radio stations make ready for the crowning of the new king. The novel does not spell out the differences between the writer of novels and the scribbler of soap-opera plots.

The Author and the Mock Autobiography

In this novel Vargas Llosa plays a point/counterpoint game between the autobiographical episodes and the fables of soap opera, as if they were two veins of a single discourse engaged in mutual imitation. It has been noted already that Aunt Julia observes that her own love affair with Marito belongs in a Camacho plot. And even though the reader is invited to read the autobiographical chapters within the conventions of realism, it is impossible to forget that both narrative tracks and modalities are in fact the writing of one single imagination and craft. Thus, the difference between the writer Mario Vargas Llosa and the scribbler Camacho clearly becomes only part of the total fictional pact of the novel. The difference between Camacho and the author exists, in fact, in the historical space beyond the text, for we as readers know that

Vargas Llosa does know how to keep up with nine or more plot lines without losing his mind. The continuity and fixed identity of the author of the novel, his sanity, resides in many more facts than the autobiographical adventures of Marito, and these are not part of the novel's story. Moreover, although the author's name coincides with the hero of the novel, it is far from being the person of Mario Vargas Llosa. And so the "author" is simply yet another fiction that operates within the novel's parody of the autobiographical pact. *Aunt Julia and the Scriptwriter* is, therefore, not an autobiographical novel but a mock autobiography. The identity of the author of the novel encompasses both Marito and Camacho. Thus, it is as if Marito/Camacho, like Alberto/the Poet and Santiago/Zavalita, were simply the two faces of the same medallion. This is further corroborated in the novel's text when Camacho brings into his plots characters from other fictions written by Vargas Llosa: Lituma/Lituma, the naked black man/Ambrosio, the Evangelist preacher/the Brother of the Arch, Sinchi/El gran Pablito, Sarita/Lalita.

There are several other levels at which the surface and mechanical point/counterpoint arrangement of the mock autobiography and the radio soap operas find points of continuity. The nine episodes in Marito's life and the eleven inconclusive plots all parody the sentimental novel. All twenty episodes tell family stories triangulated on the basis of transgressions of the kinship code, that in turn harbor the transgression of the identity code predicated by kinship. Marito, the adolescent son, grandson, and nephew in the Llosa family, becomes Varguitas, the independent husband and brother-in-law by virtue of his marriage to his aunt

Julia. Upon his return from Paris, and by virtue of his marriage to cousin Patricia and his success as a novelist, Varguitas becomes Mario Vargas Llosa, grandson of the same grandfather, son and nephew-in-law of his father and mother, nephew and son-in-law of his Uncle Lucho and his Aunt Olga, and former husband of his aunt Julia Urquidi. The character's permutating relations and identity as Marito/Varguitas/Vargas Llosa within his extended family are not only predicated by the matrimonial relations between him and two generations of females within the extended family, but also rest upon the transformation given in the trajectory of the character's occupation. Marito moves from his early journalistic days, past the days of Varguitas and the travails of his writer's apprenticeship, into the days of glory as the full-time writer of novels.

In contrast, the triangular incestuous relations that form the plots in Camacho's imagination seem incapable of passing through a similar type of transformation. Elianita's permutations make her her brother's lover and her uncle's lover, but her marriage—that is, her passage out of the family's possible kinship permutations—proves an impossibility. Thus Elianita remains within the circle of incest, remaining sister to Richard and niece to Dr. Quintero, unable to engage in exogamous sexual relations and to pass from one patriarchal circle to another. The other Elianita, Marito's other aunt, passes out of the family circle by way of her marriage to a man of Chinese ancestry. This however, proves to be a one-way trip, for her marriage entails crossing not only the circle of fire surrounding the family but also the circle of fire drawn around the confines of race. Her ostracism and her change in identity are irremediable. Elianita can never return to the Llosa family. She will belong forever to the netherworld of the "others." In a similar vein, Sarita Huanca's real or imaginary rape places the adolescent in a new, irreversible, situation. The man accused of raping her does not offer to marry her, but rather fantasizes his own self-castration as punishment for the alleged crime. Sarita describes the rape in such erotic detail that the judge in charge of discerning the truth and adjudicating justice feels aroused by the Lolita-like brief autobiography. Her parents seem interested only in finding a way to marry her off so that her sexual activity will transform the child into an adult. But alas, Sarita too remains confined within the circle of the parental family, for Gumercindo Tello's self-castration would prevent the exodus of the girl from one family into another.

In reverse order, the sexual relation between Brother Crisanto Maravillas and Sor Fátima, a sacrilegious but exogamous sexual relation, is transformed into an incestuous union by virtue of the "brother" and "sister" appellations of the religious orders. All of these sexual relations, unlike those of Marito/Varguitas/Vargas Llosa-Aunt Julia/Patricia, fail to provide the bridge by which the characters could journey from the sphere of the family romance into the world of social or public life. This is why Camacho's world of incest, infanticide, and rape ends catastrophically. It proves unable to cope with radical identity and kinship transformation. Only the world of the Llosa family can sustain such permutations; and this may be because the key transgressors self-exile themselves from Lima, the scene of the crimes, to return some ten years later fully fleshed into their new, defiant, and triumphant public selves.

The two worlds of *Aunt Julia and the Scriptwriter* also merge in the picaresque quality that marks the life not only of Pedro Camacho but also of Marito/Varguitas as the apprentice to the scriptwriter. Once again, as with *The Time of the Hero,* the originally proposed title for the novel provides an initial clue to its general meaning. Vargas Llosa has indicated that before *Aunt Julia and the Scriptwriter* became the title for the satirical experiment, he had thought of *La vida y milagros de Pedro Camacho* (The life and miracles of Pedro Camacho) as the best description for his story.[6] Any reader familiar with the Spanish Golden Age can read echoes of *El Lazarillo de Tormes, Guzmán de Alfarache,* Quevedo's *Buscoń* and even Cervantes' *Pedro de Urdemalas* in the novel's abandoned title. A reference to Pedro Camacho's opulent wedding in *Don Quixote* ("Las bodas de Camacho") is also brought in as a departure point for an intertextual reading. Geisdorfer Feal has shown how both the mock autobiography of the "author"—that is, the life of Marito/Varguitas/Vargas Llosa—and the life and plots of Pedro Camacho coincide pointedly with almost all of the essential features of the picaresque novel as outlined by Claudio Guillén and Harry Sieber.[7]

Because Marito lives with his grandparents rather than with his parents, we may consider him an orphan, a social and familial status essential in the picaresque code. Like Lázaro, his literary predecessor in *El Lazarillo de Tormes,* Marito earns his pocket money newscasting in a radio station, an insignificant job that nevertheless bears a pompous title. Like the occupation of other *pícaros,* his job entails the theft, reassembly, and rewriting of news bits from newspapers and magazines. Later on this young man of many trades tries to hold on to nine different jobs in a failed attempt to support himself and his new wife. Like other *pícaros* (for example, the Periquillo Sarniento) Marito is an old adolescent traveling across the many horizontal sectors of society and aspiring to climb up in the hierarchical distribution of posts, wealth, and privilege that holds that society in place. Like Lázaro, once at the pinnacle of all success, the social apprentice writes that he is writing an autobiography. While the autobiographic pact requires that the author writing coincide in name with the central character of the story, in *Aunt Julia and the Scriptwriter,* as in the picaresque novel, this pact is mocked. The *pícaro* writes about what he has done. He does not write about what he has been. The *pícaro* writes a mock confession in which his life is lived in imitation (mocking imitation, if you will) of the models that society has placed before him. He has not lived in response to a constant and unmitigated self-examination. The writing self-mocks the younger, now written self, but does not assail or scrutinize it from the point of view of a truly wiser man. The *pícaro* who authors his own autobiography half embraces virtue by recollecting very selectively, but writing in order to satirize all masquerading and imitation of self-identity and virtue.

Finally, in *Aunt Julia and the Scriptwriter,* Vargas Llosa goes well beyond the picaresque autobiography and engages in yet another problem of narrative representation. For the first time he includes in his fictional text the names of real people. In fact, Vargas Llosa's realism is so daring and self-assured that he does not bother to pass his characters through the elemental rite of fictional baptism. The illusion of fiction here pretends not to have passed through the accustomed filters of fictionalization. The novel keeps—almost flaunts—the real-life people with their actual historical names, in the same city, at the same historical time, and even at their own addresses. The entire mock autobiography relies heavily on the pseudohistorical presentation of the Llosa family, which, of course, stands in contrast with the fictional names given to Camacho's characters and Camacho himself. Camacho's real name seems to have been Raúl Salomón. It is precisely the exaggerated realism articulated in the real names, dates, and places that provokes Julia Urquidi's disclaimers in *Lo que Varguitas no dijo.*[8] The novel thus contains, all at once, many possibilities for reading and interpreting its daring mix of chronicle, mock autobiography, realistic novel, and parody of the sentimental romance.

NOTES

1. See Sara Castro-Klarén, "Humor and Class in *Pantaleón y las visitadoras,*" *The Latin American Literary Review* (Fall-Winter 1978) 64–79. *Huachafo* means a large number of things in colloquial speech in Peru. Basically, it refers to feeling socially and racially superior to others. The *huachafo* is faulted for misinterpreting the styles and characteristics of his betters in the desire to emulate them.

2. *Cholo:* a person of any race, color, creed, or social status regarded by the criollo/speaker as someone improperly initiated into the symbolic code of being the master, that is, the person who understands the duplicity of the given local situation.

3. Marta Morello-Frosch "Of Heroes and Martyrs: The Grotesque in *Pantaleón y las visitadoras,*" *Latin American Literary Review* (Spring-Summer 1979) 42–43.

4. Ricardo Cano Gaviria, *El buitre y el ave fénix: Conversaciones con Mario Vargas Llosa* (Barcelona: Anagrama, 1972) 90–92. The translation is mine.

5. Mario Vargas Llosa, *La tía Julia y el escribidor,* 5th ed. (Barcelona: Seix Barral, 1983) 276. All translations are mine, and page numbers are given in parentheses.

6. José Miguel Oviedo, "Conversación con Mario Vargas Llosa sobre *La tía Julia y el escribidor,*" in *Mario Vargas Llosa: A Collection of Critical Essays,* ed. Charles Rossman and Alan Warren Friedman, (Austin: University of Texas Press, 1978) 158.

7. Rosemary Geisdorfer Feal, *Novel Lives: The Fictional Autobiographies of Guillermo Cabera Infante and Mario Vargas Llosa* (Chapel Hill: University of North Carolina Department of Romance Languages, 1986).

8. Julia Urquidi Illánez, *Lo que Varguitas no dijo,* (La Paz, Khana Cruz: Biblioteca Popular Boliviana de Ultima Hora, 1983).

CHAPTER SEVEN

Cinematography and *The War of the End of the World*

In many of the interviews given by Mario Vargas Llosa since the publication of his first novel, *The Time of the Hero,* he has freely spoken of himself as a dedicated and voracious movie fan and of the influence that cinema has had on his narrative strategies. In the chapter on *The Green House,* thanks to the painstaking critical work of Luis A. Diez, we have endeavored to show how many of Vargas Llosa's narrative innovations are closely linked to the speed and montage of cinematographic narrative. His interest in the melodramatic side of Mexican blockbuster movies has also been documented in the truculent and even grotesque configuration of the characters and stories of *Captain Pantoja and the Special Service* and *Aunt Julia and the Scriptwriter.*

In 1973 the Brazilian movie director Rui Guerra was planning to make a film based on the classical Brazilian essay *Os Sertões* (1903 [*Rebellion in the Backlands,* 1944]), by Euclides da Cunha. Rui Guerra asked Mario Vargas Llosa to read the voluminous historical essay on the civil war that plagued northeastern Brazil during the last decade of the nineteenth century and to write a script for a screen version. So, as he had previously done in preparation for writing and creating jungle scenarios for *The Green House,* Vargas Llosa traveled to the backlands of northeastern Brazil. He read widely about its history, its flora and fauna. In the backlands of Bahia he met the local folk, spoke at length with those who still remembered something about the days of the war, the legends surrounding the Conselheiro, and the fabulous bandits of the *sertão.* The purpose of this trip was to nourish and set the parameters of the imaginary world that would emerge in his movie script.

Just as in the earlier case of the jungle setting for *The Green House,* Vargas Llosa must have found out that there was already a vigorous literary tradition about the backlands of Bahia, Ceará, and the other states comprising the Brazilian northeast. Da Cunha's master narrative is perhaps only the most brilliant and best known of a large number of travelogues, novels, essays, and *crónicas* of the *sertâo.* In spite of Rui Guerra's interest in making the movie and Vargas Llosa's willingness to engage in necessary documentary preparation to write the script, the project failed. The movie was not made.

In 1976, however, a movie based on *Captain Pantoja* and made in the Dominican Republic was released in the Spanish-speaking world. Mario Vargas Llosa was involved in the production and direction of the movie, which not only follows Pantoja's adventures but resembles in tone and feeling the radio soap operas and movies made in Cuba before the Fidel Castro revolution of 1959. The movie became a hit with the same mass audience that Vargas Llosa fictionalized in *Aunt Julia and the Scriptwriter.* Soon after the controversial success of his satirical *Aunt Julia,* Marito's mock autobiography was serialized by a Colombian radio station. Scandalized and resentful of what she described as invasion of privacy, Julia Urquidi sued the Colombian producers in an effort to stop airing of the soap opera about "her life." In 1986, under the direction of the young Peruvian director Francisco Lombardi Perry and with mostly an amateur cast, a sober and excellent adaptation of *The Time of the Hero* was released to critical acclaim.

Vargas Llosa explores the world of mass communication as either journalism or radio soap opera in *Conversation in The Cathedral, Captain Pantoja,* and *Aunt Julia*. At the same time, however, he explores the relation of historical discourse to fiction. In *Aunt Julia* we see how daringly and deftly he retains the historical names of his characters, who in the fictional world represent the members of his family; and at the same time marks the whole discourse and story of the novel with the clear color of the mock autobiography and parody. On the one hand, the writer seems to have drawn nearer to the conventions of journalistic reporting; on the other hand, he seems to erase all these conventions, to write over them the differential marking of fiction. The Llosa family appears placed squarely in the realm of realism, that is, a space of social existence and action subject to verification outside the text of the novel. However, the information given on each member of the family—barely a name and kinship placement—is so scant as to render the aunts, uncles, cousins, and grandparents as mere vehicles for a plot in which what matters is, once again, action and not character, kinship relations and not individual passions. With the possible exception of

Camacho, all characters in *Aunt Julia* appear as disembodied relations—family relations—that make possible the incestuous and truculent liaisons weaving the plot.

Action and the Apocalypse

A few years after Vargas Llosa's first visit to the backlands of the Brazilian northeast, the Peruvian novelist went back to Brazil for further documentation on Euclides da Cunha's work and the rebellion in Canudos. This time he seems to have read the diary that Euclides da Cunha wrote during the months when he, as a correspondent for a major Brazilian newspaper, reported on the war. Vargas Llosa also read newspapers of the period. All of this was in preparation for the writing of his novel on the Conselheiro's messianic movement, *La guerra del fin del mundo* (1981 [*The War of the End of the World,* 1984]). The novel was awarded the first annual Ritz Paris Hemingway Prize in 1985.

This huge novel depicts the chilling and fabulous adventures of a large number of characters caught in the deep social upheaval that took place in the backlands of Bahia shortly after Brazil became an independent republic. Without the anticipation of anyone involved in this dispute among the conservative peasant-*lumpen* masses, Bahia's regional urban political forces, and Rio de Janeiro's weak central government, the conflict quickly evolved into a civil war of apocalyptic contours. The scenes in which the protracted armed struggle for the defense of Canudos is depicted appear taken right out of Hollywood's biblical and Western sagas or pirate movies. Bodies in repose, in agony, and in swift, maddening motion constitute the mainstay of this novel. The opening of the camera lens is almost always wide and in close-up to better capture the body's movement, its extraordinary gymnastic ability, the contortions of a face in pain, the silent gesturing of men and women in the midst of battle. Point of view on the canvas is almost always internal, as if the narrator, like God, managed to be intimately present in all the thousands of locales and scenes where the simultaneous actions take place. For example, the long-awaited first assault of the Brazilian army upon the *lumpen* assembled in Canudos is depicted from within the midst of the square of the town under siege:

> Upon returning, Maria Quadrado managed to get close to João Grande, and when she was about to tell him that the Leon de Natuba was missing, the first cannon blast was heard. The multitude stopped and listened. Many, confused, explored the sky. But another cannon blast thundered, and they saw one of the hovels by the cemetery explode in splinters and red-hot coals. . . . João Abade gave orders to put out the candles and wick lamps in Canudos. Soon the city became a dark pit.[1]

The story of the war is narrated in a relentless sequence of scenes of violence and dazzling action interrupted only by moments of sheer physical exhaustion. After the battle there is always a moment of rest. The combatants spared from death or mutilation look after the sick, the dying, and the starving, only to start fighting again when they least expect it, for this is a guerrilla war waged principally by the element of surprise. Sometimes the fighters themselves seem surprised by their own determination to risk it all in a moment of despair. Each combatant becomes a veritable war machine interested only in his enemy's annihilation. Death, one's own final physical end, appears meaningless in contrast with the idea of killing the other. In a masterful scene in which one man's physical and mental courage is rendered, we see encapsulated the sanguinary and apocalyptic nature of the "final solution" that razes Canudos to the ground:

> He looks, and sees horsemen with lances. Two hundred, many more. They have crossed the Vassa Barris, half a kilometer to his right. They are forming up in platoons so as to attack the lower flank under the bugle's frenetic sound.... In a second, he sees what's going to happen. The lancers ... will reach Belo Monte in a few minutes. Once they discover the opening, the soldiers will follow. Neither Pedrão, nor João Grande, nor Pajeú has had time to fall back to the city to reinforce the *jaguncos* hidden behind the roofs and towers of churches.... Then, without knowing what he is going to do, guided only by the madness of the moment, he grabs his munition bag, jumps out of the pit, shouting to Honorio: "We've got to stop them, follow me, follow me." He runs, his head low, the Mannlincher on his right side, the revolver to his left side, the bag over one shoulder, feeling like a dream.... At that moment, the fear of death—which sometimes wakes him up in a cold sweat, or freezes his blood in the middle of a trivial conversation—disappears, and what overcomes him is a sovereign contempt for the idea of being wounded or disappearing from the realm of the living (443).

While captivating the reader with the events and outcome of the story, *The War of the End of the World* offers and demands a reading beyond and beneath the plot. This conjugation of hundreds of characters caught in moments of critical decisions, conversions, and self-revelations delves into problems that Vargas Llosa has grappled with before: religious fanaticism, political corruption and self-delusion, the unbearable weight of fossilized ideologies or utopias, the absurdity of sensational journalism, sexual excess and experimentation, faith, hunger, and fraternal love. None of the more than forty-three lives chronicled in the novel conclude in marriage, death, or exile from the community in which the drama is set, as they would in a realistic novel. Individuals see their lives brought to end by the war, by an inexorable death that does not leave behind a community in which the consequences of their living and dying can be felt or measured. There are no wills, no heirs, no family left to mourn the dead. Only the scorched earth remains as witness of the blood spilled in Canudos. The ending of *The War of the End of the World,* unlike Vargas Llosa's previous ambiguous endings, is final and unequivocal for the Conselheiro's followers, for many soldiers, for Galileo Gall, and for General Moreira César. For those who go on, people like the Barão de Canhabrava, the journalist of *O Journal de Noticias,* and the high echelons of the Brazilian army, life will never be the same after the apocalypse at Canudos. Even though Vargas Llosa has added only a few characters to Euclides da Cunha's rendition of the war, and remains faithful to the main historical events of the last decade of the nineteenth century, one of the chief differences between *Os*

Sertões and *The War of the End of the World* is the uncompromising apocalyptic tenor of the novel.

The Dualistic Structure Revisited: Canudos and Bahia

As we have seen in several of his previous novels, Vargas Llosa deploys the events of his story along the lines of two separate geographic and social riverbanks. In the case of *The War of the End of the World,* only a few characters cross from one side to the other; and even fewer return. Jurema and the journalist cross from the Bahia urban sphere to Canudos. Having been miraculously spared, they return to life in Bahia after the war is over. Galileo Gall, a utopian European, embarks on a spiritual journey to the Conselheiro's first settlement. He reaches Canudos when the plantation still belongs to the Barão. The European anarchist never really makes it to the Canudos of the social experiment and apocalypse. With the exception of the Conselheiro during his very early days, no one from the backlands ever reaches Bahia or returns to Monte Belo, Uãuà, or Canudos. The Brazilian army, of course, makes it to Canudos, destroys it, and, itself tattered and almost defeated, returns to the barracks of the republic.

Each side has its own social logic and history from which characters and events are generated for the story of the war. As the action of the novel progresses, the lives of characters anchored on either side begin to project a shadow and a desire that reaches beyond the chasm that keeps them separated. The body of the novel grows as if a weaver at the loom had begun taking threads from one side in order to mix their colors with the threads from the other side. The chapters and sections that integrate the novel almost mechanically alternate a section set in the backlands with a section set in Bahia, with yet another section focused on either the army's or Galileo Gall's march to Canudos. *The War of the End of the World* is thus structured in the form of a double spiral: Bahia/sertão, city/countryside, Barão/Conselheiro, jagunços/republican army, messianism/republican civilian ideology.

What happens in the backlands towns of Bahia, the singular and privileged focus in Euclides da Cunha's historical essay, is balanced, or rather flanked, by the political events and discourse set in Bahia. Galileo Gall, the romantic European phrenologist, is perhaps one of the most idiosyncratic and weak characters added to the original story on the side of Bahia. The Barão, an important character in *The War of the End of the World,* can only be implied in *Os Sertões,* even though the Barão de Canhabrava is probably based on the historical Barão de Gerembão. Gonçalvez Viana, although a historical participant in the events of Bahia, appears to be a composite of the various self-serving and vain Bahian politicians who saw in the Conselheiro's following the excuse to attack their enemies and consolidate the new republican power.

Critics have been quick to point out that since Euclides da Cunha was the journalist who accompanied the troops and, with reports that he wired to his newspaper, created the furor that this expedition actually caused in Brazil, Vargas Llosa's myopic journalist has a historical referent in Euclides da Cunha. If this is so, then *La guerra del fin del mundo* parodies not only utopian and idealistic figures such as Gall but also the best and most committed Latin American intellectuals. Because of the great distance in intellectual prowess and quality between da Cunha and the journalist in this novel, I am inclined to think that the latter has no specific historical referent.

Even though the bespectacled, flabby journalist cannot be assigned any specific equivalent in history, his soft physique and stubborn intellectual demeanor seem to place him within a general scheme that Vargas Llosa uses for his journalists, scriblers, or well-intentioned souls such as Mayta in *The Real Life of Alejandro Mayta,* Pedro Camacho in *Aunt Julia,* or even Saúl Zurata in *El hablador*. These little men are singled out by an unmistakable physical defect: myopia, a birthmark, standing red hair, flat feet, or a big soft belly. As if to compensate for their physical disability, these little men have learned to endure physical pain and humiliation. Moreover, they are indefatigable in their moral and intellectual pursuits, a quality that makes them carriers of a terrible disease: the questioning of established modes of perception, the desire to halt the common contempt for the poor and suffering, along with an intrinsic solidarity with such "marginal" peoples. Thus, in *The War of the End of the World,* Galileo Gall is not far apart from the myopic journalist, nor is he too far away from the nearly anthropomorphic body of the León de Natuba, or the Dwarf, or even the epileptic body of Moreira César. These monstrous little men stand in sheer contrast with the natural and at the same time studied elegance and perfect physique of the cultivated Barão and the army engineer who reconnoiters and maps the route for the Brazilian troops advancing upon Canudos. The latter is more likely to stand as the fictional version of Euclides da Cunha who before taking up journalism had been a military engineer.

With the exception of *Who Killed Palomino Molero?* this vast novel can be said to be the most traditional in Vargas Llosa's oeuvre. Each character is presented in a sort of careful block of portrayal. After the initial physical and social presentation of the characters, what evolves is a set of minor traits as the characters respond to the extraordinary circumstances in which they find themselves. Indirect interior monologue is often used to unveil the individual's mind before he or she faces the possibility of death, the certainty of physical pain, or the shaking doubt and weakness felt before the killing of a fellow human being. But even though this critical moment is subtly scrutinized in the cases of Maria Quadrado, Pedrão, João Grande, Pajeú, Rufino, and many others, the particulars of the case do not seem fundamentally different in each character's crisis. Nor do they seem to stem from the past of each different person in crisis. In fact, each moment of truth in this tale of killing and maiming seems to be more a variation on the same theme than an indepth, sustained examination of a single personality before his or her transgression. There is no Raskolnikov in either the character or the plot dynamics of *The War of the End of the World*. Death and murder fall upon people with too great a speed. Death and murder are not the subjects of intense and extensive meditation as in *Crime and Punishment*. In this war death and murder seem inexorable. Characters do not have the time or inclination to consider either at great length.

Death, violent death, is simply a given of life. There is only time to feel the shudder of fear and then face up to the inevitable. Maria Quadrado's anguished consciousness in search of an almost unattainable good is often portrayed in the days before the first assault on Canudos. She unfolds the pleats of her fear as a rebuke to her inability to feel happy before the end:

> She would have to be happy, because this means that the suffering of the body will come to an end, that she would see the Father and the Holy Trinity, thought Maria Quadrado. But fear permeated her. She begged God to forgive her cowardice, and she tried to pray. . . . But she could not concentrate her mind on the Credo. João Abade and João Grande no longer insisted in taking him [the Conselheiro] to the refuge. The Commander of Streets tried to persuade him not to visit the trenches: the war could surprise him in the open air, without any protection whatsoever, Father (284–85).

Part of the richness of the novel stems from the portrayal of characters during self-examination. Moments of indirect interior monologue dot the telling of the story, offering a contrapuntal relation between the depiction of physical action and the unveiling of consciousness. The Beatito and the León de Natuba, together with Maria Quadrado, are the characters closest to the Conselheiro and to the flow of spiritual energy that emanates from his person and his silence. In search of sainthood and the understanding of their good fortune, the León de Natuba questions his frail faith, weak love, and self-loathing:

> He was unfair. Not only did he owe thanks to the Counselor, but also to the others. Did they not carry him when he no longer had the strength [to walk]? Did they not pray, especially the Beatito, so that he could have faith? Was Maria Quadrado not kind and generous toward him? He tried to think with love of the Mother of Men. She had tried her best to get him to like her. . . . When he had had the fevers, she had cuddled him in her arms to give him warmth. . . . Why then, did he not love her? No doubt, because [he] had heard her accuse herself and confess her feeling of disgust for the Leon de Natuba and her belief that his ugliness was the work of the Evil One. . . . I am spiteful, he thought (258).

In this vast epic the characters enjoy a greater stability than in *Aunt Julia* or *The Green House*. No radical changes in identity occur. There are no characters whose life seems to have come to a novelistic end in one story (Bonifacia), only to reappear in another under a different name (Selvática). Even though many of the characters in the backlands side of the story experience a great spiritual crisis before becoming the Conselheiro's followers, once they see the light and make a vow, they are set forever in their new profile. This conversion is seldom portrayed fully; it just seems to happen, as if the poor, the forgotten, the bandits, and the criminals who swell Antonio Conselheiro's ranks had been living their lives in expectation of the one moment of revelation. Such is the picture of Maria Quadrado's appearance in Monte Santo, the Conselheiro's first settlement:

> She appeared one rainless dawn, high on the road to Quijingue. She was carrying a cross on her back. She

> was twenty years old, but she had suffered so much that she looked ancient. She was a broad-faced woman, with bruised feet, a shapeless body, and mouse-colored skin. Her name was Maria Quadrado, and she had walked from Salvador to Monte Santo. She had borne the cross for three months and a day.... Her head was a patchwork of bare skull and stiff locks of hair that reminded people of the lunatics in the Salvador asylum. She had shaved her head after having been raped for the fourth time (49).

Just as in *Os Sertões,* the Conselheiro's following in this novel encompasses all kinds of outlaws, fools, disabled, hungry, killers, renegade priests, and even itinerant merchants of the backlands. Buried deeply in their marginal, deprived, and suffering lives, the reason for their conversion vibrates unknown but alive. In contrast to da Cunha's version of the Conselheiro's person and message—"the babblings of a fool or a madman"—Vargas Llosa's rendition of the messianic and charismatic Conselheiro remains enshrouded in mystery and silence.[2] His beliefs, his very early Christian version of the message of Galilee, appears in the novel as part of the Beatito's search for the Conselheiro's word, Maria Quadrado's quest for repentance, and the León de Natuba's quest for humanity in the Conselheiro's loving acceptance of his deformed and repugnant body. The Conselheiro's indirect message appears to be a strange mixture of love and wrath, compassion and vengeance, hope in the Good Jesus and the expectation of the cleansing, final scorching of a corrupt and mean world. His hope is messianic, for the social and material hold only the despair of the same ancient hunger and suffering.

Story and Discourse: The Conselheiro, the Republic, and War

In the fictionalized version of the historical Conselheiro that *The War of the End of the World* describes, the man who appears for the first time in Monte Santo is a shadowy, unworldly figure. The first scenes that introduce the character project a poor, humble lay brother who moves from one miserable town to another, rebuilding fallen cemetery walls and abandoned churches. Extremely ascetic, the dirty and silent lay brother lives exclusively on the meager alms—food and drink—that the possible parishioners of the abandoned churches bring him. He never asks for anything. He refuses all but the most frugal meal.

After a long time of roaming the desert, the man seems moved to speak. He begins to preach in the atriums of the churches that he and a few volunteers cleaned up and rebuilt. The Conselheiro preaches the need for repentance for the great sins that people commit daily. Repentance is necessary immediately, for the end of the world is at hand. To the Conselheiro and the people of the *sertão* (backlands) who listen to him, the end of the world is the time of great deliverance. At last, deliverance from suffering can be a real hope. The possibility of a great rest for the exhausted land and the equally spent *sertanejos* now seems to be real. The Conselheiro's preaching holds, as the final reward for repentance, repose and peace. Union.with sweet

Jesus seems to be their idea of final bliss and eternal reward.

Slowly and imperceptibly the Conselheiro's preaching begins to attract followers. He does not ask people to join him, he does not really instruct them. They simply join him, hang around him at night, share the alms that they are offered. Without a plan the poor, the vagabonds, and other outcasts and pilgrims become a solidarian community. Breaking his habitual silence, perhaps his long meditation, the Conselheiro erupts, from time to time, into fiery sermons about the coming of the end of the world, the end of the reign of all those who have abandoned Christ and his laws, laws that the Conselheiro affirms above any human law.

The Conselheiro's following grows larger almost imperceptibly. One day the authorities of nearby towns and churches awake to realize that the Conselheiro's adherence to Jesus' supreme law represents a challenge to their own worldly interests and power. Many people in the towns feel empowered to challenge the supreme power of the police, the local mayor, or the local priest. The potential conflict between civilian rulers and the Conselheiro's religious preaching soon comes to a head with the proclamation of the republic's new laws. While the empire had ruled the interior of Brazil negligently, the new republic aggressively seeks to stretch its rule and power over the entire territory outlined as the sovereign space for the new nation. Many of the laws proclaimed by the new state do not make any sense in the *sertão;* what is more, they go against the mores and age-old customs of the backlands people.

Seeing that the Conselheiro attracts people to mass,

baptism, and even marriage, many of the local priests, who have in turn been forgotten and abandoned by their dioceses, allow him to do his preaching in church atriums. The priests are nervous about his preaching, but happy to collect a few coins for the dispensation of the sacraments. Things begin to change, however, when the Conselheiro, in his parsimonious but irrevocable way, indicates that he wants to preach—to "his" lambs—inside the churches and from the pulpit. A few priests are willing to bend even here, but many others see a tremendous danger in lending the Conselheiro the trappings and symbols of their authority and monopoly over the sacred. This parting of the ways between some local priests and the Conselheiro more or less coincides with the aggressive promulgation of the new laws of the republic. Hostility between the church's hierarchy and the Conselheiro grows. He becomes despondent and loses no time in showing his contempt for the church and its sins. Keeping a watchful eye over the Conselheiro's relations with the church, the guardians of civilian power and authority grow restless and nervous every time the Conselheiro and his large following arrive in the outskirts of a town in the *sertão*.

The news of his presence in the desert reaches Bahia. Bishop, journalists, lawyers, governor, and landowners think that the man's influence on the "unthinking" *lumpen* should be contained and watched over carefully. Thus, a detachment of soldiers is ordered to make its way into the *sertão* to arrest the man. His followers, many of whom suspect the government's ill intentions and, in anticipation, have set up a net of spies, find out about the arrest order long before the soldiers get to the *sertão*. In their minds this confirms the inimical attitude of the government and the alliance of the republic with the devil himself. The Conselheiro's followers decide to take the initiative.

In *Os Sertões,* Euclides da Cunha implies that the Conselheiro is the mastermind behind the deeds of his followers. In *The War of the End of the World,* however, he appears as a vague figure whose desires and orders are more divined by his followers than explicitly given by the mystic himself. It stands to reason that the Conselheiro should wish not to be arrested. But he does not say so at any moment, nor does the text of the novel indicate that he is aware of the government's plans for him. It is his followers who interpret, and take the step that links interpretation of "the Word" to consequent action upon the world. Later, in Canudos, we shall be puzzled once again by the Conselheiro's mystical and silent body, in contrast with his followers' clever determination to build the citadel and defend it and their salvation with all their might and ferocity. How the Conselheiro's silence, or vague references to the Dog/Devil or to sweet Jesus, is translated into such specific historical action remains a mystery and a weak point in the discourse of the novel.

As the soldiers nervously approach one of the lost towns of the *sertão* where the Conselheiro's guard has laid its trap, the first battle between the Brazilian messianic rabble and the Brazilian armed forces surerupts. Because of the darkness, the element of surprise, and their clarity of conviction, the Conselheiro's wretched bunch of men and women score their first victory. Even though they suffer many losses, the Conselheiro's people, accustomed to the idea of battles between the *coroneis's* private armies and the *cangaceiros* and other armed groups in the *sertão,* thank the good Lord Jesus and take their victory in stride. They know, however, that this is only the first battle in a protracted but not really new war between the government's forces and the various resisting forces of the *sertão*.

In *The War of the End of the World* the victory of the Conselheiro's rabble over the soldiers is distinctly attributed to the planning strategy and flawless execution of the battle plan conceived by the former bandits or *cangaceiros* joining the Conselheiro's following. Certainly such a view of the Conselheiro as the head of an army of bandits is the prevailing belief in the thinking minds of Bahia. In the educated circles of that town it is believed that the Conselheiro, posing as a mystic, works in fact as an agent for infamous England in her interest to destabilize the fledging Brazilian republic. The frightened and self-righteous Bahians tell each other that only England's might, her capacity to finance and arm colonial wars, could account for the Conselheiro's victory over a detachment of Brazilian soldiers. The Conselheiro must be destroyed. He is a threat to the entire nation. The central government in Rio must be made to see the danger and send the Brazilian army to defeat this intolerable rebellion. After all, the Brazilian army, victorious against Paraguay in the War of the Triple Alliance fought by Argentina, Uruguay, and Brazil against Paraguay in 1864, knows exactly how to deal with backlands people. In the minds of the Bahian politicians and the emerging bourgeoisie that they represent the solution seems at hand.

Back in the desert the Conselheiro and his followers keep on roaming in search of a natural castle, a place from which they can organize their defense. The choice is difficult in view of the fact that the number of people who arrive daily to join the Conselheiro's followers grows continually. It is as if all the downtrodden of the huge Brazilian *sertão* were congregating at the feet of this compassionate but single-minded man who has nothing to offer but love and eternal salvation. Natural leaders, many of them famous and feared bandits, begin to emerge as the Conselheiro's lieutenants. Pedrão, João Abade, João Grande, Pajeú, the Villanova brothers, the Sardelinha sisters, and Maria Quadrado become the founders of a new order in Canudos, the place finally chosen for the Conselheiro's experimental creation of a Christian community.

Canudos is chosen because, in contrast with the rest of the many other possible sites, it has water year round. The former site of the Barão de Canhabrava's plantation, Canudos sits on the banks of the Vassa Barris river. The Canudos abandoned plantation, house, and corrals are burned to the ground, for purification purposes, as Pajeú announces to the Baroness; then the Conselheiro's people begin to settle down. Midwives, itinerant peddlers, ex-bandits, murderers, carpenters, storytellers, and all the dispossessed and scum of the earth meet in Canudos. They organize a solidarian society where enough food and dignity is the bread of daily life. This society was never described by Euclides da Cunha. Although critical of the way the army and the state eventually disposed of Canudos, and compassionate toward his fellow Brazilians, da Cunha saw absolutely no place for the Conselheiro's followers or their experiment in Brazilian national life. On a rich and detailed canvas Vargas Llosa brings to life the human quest and achievement of the rabble assembled at Canudos. Each group and person is given an unforgettable portrait. The *cangaceiros,* in their dual role as bandits and saints, form the most exotic and interesting grouping:

> They were a strange bunch of emissaries from heaven. Instead of dressing up in tunics, they wore leather shirts and pants. They were the same men: they carried shotguns, knives, and machetes; and yet, they were not the same men, because now, all they could talk about was the Counselor, God, or their place of origin. . . . Religion satisfied their days now.

Vargas Llosa chronicles the town's birth as simultaneous with the rebirth of the populace:

> As they were finished, the tortuous little streets were baptized with the name of a saint in a procession. . . . Many of the reborn changed their name in order to symbolize the beginning of their new life. . . . Human diversity coexisted in Canudos without violence, in the midst of a fraternal solidarity and an atmosphere of exaltation that the elect had never known before. They truly felt rich for being poor, children of God, privileged. This they were told every afternoon by the man with the cloak full of holes.

Not unlike the emergence of self-government in the shantytowns of Peru, chronicled by present-day sociologists, spontaneous social organization in Canudos makes its mark in creating a just human order:

In spite of the multiplication of inhabitants, life was not chaotic. The guides and pilgrims brought cattle and provisions; the corrals were full of animals. The warehouses were also brimming. Honorio and Antonio Villanova managed the city: they received offerings brought by the pilgrims, distributed clothing and food, and watched over the House of Health set up for the aging, the sick, and the orphans (92–94).

History and Genocide

Almost coinciding with the moment when Canudos emerges as a full-fledged community, the Brazilian army, led by the famous general Moreira César, starts marching toward Canudos. Four cut-throat assaults are necessary to bring Canudos down after more than a year and a half of butchery. Thousands of soldiers and civilians suffer the most painful deaths. In the end, after a few old women and children march out of the hovels left in Canudos only to be put to the knife, the citadel is burned down in yet another act of "purification." Both in da Cunha's narrative and in Vargas Llosa's rendition of the war this bloody episode passes from the silent annals of Latin American history to fill the first pages of a catalogue of genocides embedded in the civil wars that have ravaged the continent.

In *The War of the End of the World,* Vargas Llosa deploys all his narrative powers to produce an engrossing epic. For the reader the emotional charge of the story of the war in Canudos is only comparable to the suspense and identification created by the duels in *The Three Musketeers* or the battles in *War and Peace.* Even if the reader has read *Os sertões* and is familiar with the outcome of Canudos's story, Vargas Llosa's mastery of suspense creates the false illusion that, in the novel at least, the final destiny of the characters one has learned to love might not be death. Paradoxically, the reader of *Os Sertões* finds himself hoping that in *The War of the End of the World* Pajeú will emerge alive from his final suicidal mission. The same reader hopes against hope that the Brazilian army might encounter yet another insurmountable obstacle, and thus retreat before leveling Canudos. The force of the reality created in the fictional text is so great as to provoke in the reader the childlike desire that the world brought to life in the act of reading might endure beyond the final page and beyond the last period of the novel.

Once the magic of the first reading is over, one can see clearly that the power of the story set in the *sertão* overwhelms its counterpart set in Bahia. While the *sertão* appears to be populated by people sincere and spontaneous, even in their revenge and cruelty, Bahia contains characters fraught with hypocrisy and self-delusion. Some of the Bahian characters, Gonçalvez Viana, and the journalist Galileo Gall, are reminiscent of the world of *Aunt Julia and the Scriptwriter.* While the Barão has been considered by some to be the central character in the novel, others find in him too many gratuitous contradictions. It is not easy to reconcile a facile retreat from Bahian politics in a man who along with his family has played a major role in the power game of the state. The sober and elegant owner of Canudos is not quite convincing in his ascetic views on the burning of his family plantation, or in the contained depression over his wife's madness. At the same time that he retreats from politics, merely laments his wife's illness, and passes over the loss of his estate, he seems to find an incongruous satisfaction in watching the chameleon that inhabits his indoor garden and raping his wife's chambermaid in the presence of his "beloved" Baroness. Somehow, the Barão's asceticism does not manage to compete with the physical exploits and the faith that nourishes the acts of Pajeú or the Villanova brothers. The final interpretation of the war and its raison d'être is left in the text to the Barão. Upon his return from Europe, and at the request of the surviving, myopic journalist, the Barão attempts to satisfy the journalist's curious and puzzled reasoning with the idea that there are some things in history that just don't make any sense. The butchery at Canudos is one of those events beyond reason. The Barão proposes that, rather than ponder this war's meaning, it is best to forget. Such final words weaken not only the image of the Barão as a principal and highly educated person in the story, but also the coherence of the discourse emerging from the entire corpus of the novelistic text. The Barão's studied distance from the immediate history of Bahia and Brazil comes as a weak epilogue in light of the novel's historical force:

> "Now I remember," said the Baron. "Someone wrote me that you were alive. I found out while in Europe. 'A ghost appeared.' Someone wrote me that. But in spite of that, I continued to believe that you were dead, that you had disappeared."
>
> "I did not die and I did not disappear," a little nasal voice said.
>
> "Canudos?" said the Baron. "Epaminondas is right in wishing that people wouldn't talk about that

story any more. Let us forget it. That's best. It is a sad, muddy, confusing episode. It is no use. History must be instructive, exemplary. In that war, no one acted gloriously. And no one understands what happened. People have decided to draw a curtain. That's wise, healthy" (340–41).

In spite of the puzzles in the novel's discourse, *The War of the End of the World* not only retells a powerful and tragic story but also opens the vast expanses of the historical novel for Mario Vargas Llosa's work. The author's interest in history, in narrative history to be exact, dates back to his university days when he studied with the Peruvian historian Raúl Porras Barrenechea. Vargas Llosa's interest in history also dwells on the gestation of great social movements, revolutions, mutinies, and civil war, some of which have appeared already in *Conversation in The Cathedral* (the Arequipa revolt) and *Captain Pantoja* (the cult of the Brothers of the Arch). *The War of the End of the World,* however, evinces Vargas Llosa's growing interest in the relation between ideology and action. Any observer of some recent trends in Latin American societies and politics can discern the analogies between the Conselheiro's Christian messianism, his communitarian preaching, and his silent criticism of the established church, and many of the precepts and questions raised by liberation theology.

Finally, it would seem that this obsessive curiosity about history, its causes and movements, was not satiated in the writing of the story of Canudos and its diverse forms of armed struggle and organized violence. On the contrary: Vargas Llosa's interest in ideology and action (revolution and revolt)—that is, in the cultural decomposition of the structure of desire and the many surprising faces in which it can reappear—has only been stimulated with the explorative writing of this story of rebellion in the backlands. In his later novels, *The Real Life of Alejandro Mayta, Who Killed Palomino Molero?* and *El hablador,* Vargas Llosa reexamines the nature of desire, its mysterious mix with ideology, and the dynamics of the body in further episodes dealing directly with recent events in Peruvian and Latin American history.

NOTES

1. Mario Vargas Llosa, *La guerra del fin del mundo* (Barcelona: Seix Barral, 1981) 288. All translations are mine; page numbers are given in parentheses.

2. Sara Castro-Klarén, "Santos and Cangaceiros: Inscription without Discourse in *Os Sertões* and *La guerra del fin del mundo,*" *Modern Language Notes* (1986) 366–88.

CHAPTER EIGHT

Myth, Ideology, and Revolution: From Mayta to Tasurinchi

In *Historia de Mayta* (1984 [*The Real Life of Alejandro Mayta,* 1986]) we find a new emphasis on certain aspects of narrative rhetoric that initially appeared in Vargas Llosa's parodial texts. In *Aunt Julia and the Scriptwriter* and the play *La Señorita de Tacna* (1981) an explicit inquiry into the questions of writing, authorship, and the creation of fiction emerges. The binominal writer/scribbler now appears anchored in the meddlesome distinction between history and fiction, and between truth and falsehood as alternative versions of creative imagination. It is as if Little Red Riding Hood had asked the wolf: "Dear Grandmother, what is the truth for?" And the wolf had replied: "The truth helps me tell you better lies." In *The Real Life of Alejandro Mayta* the author and narrator of the story asserts that he tells lies, knowing full well the real or truthful reason for doing so. Like *Aunt Julia, The Real Life of Alejandro Mayta* also proposes a game around the nature of autobiographical writing, for the "real" Mario Vargas Llosa, the author of *The Time of the Hero,* deploys a version of himself as the main autobiographical narrator of Mayta's story. Once again in this political novel we are before the *mise-en-scène* in which the writer writes that he writes.

Vargas Llosa, unlike Julio Cortázar when he wrote his antinovel *Rayuela* (1963 [*Hopscotch,* 1966]), creates in *Aunt Julia* a mock autobiography rather than an antibiography. *In the Real Life of Alejandro Mayta,* Vargas Llosa mixes and refashions the mimetic conventions of biography, and autobiography and the political novel. Both in *La Señorita de Tacna* (The Young Lady from Tacna) and *Kathie y el hipopótamo* (1983) [Kathie and the Hippopotamus]), Vargas Llosa focuses the action of the text in characters who, like Marito or Camacho, are writers or want to be writers. In *La Señorita de Tacna* Belisario writes, possessed by the belief that writing is the only operation capable of rescuing the past, and thus the self, from the debris of forgetfulness. The main character, who also functions as the narrator of this short play, takes the occasion to meditate on and experiment with the many possible ways of telling his story. The dramatization of his story in *La Señorita de Tacna* thus becomes only one possible way of telling his story, of saving lived but by now imagined life from the gullet of a deadening past. In this sense Vargas Llosa's plays are reminiscent of Cortázar's narrative experiments with the identity and person of the narrator in his short story collection *Las armas secretas* (1964), and especially in "Las babas del diablo," later transformed by the Italian director Michelangelo Antonioni into the classic film *Blow-Up.*

In *Kathie y el hipopótamo* memory and the past are treated in the exact opposite way than in *La Señorita de Tacna,* for Kathie, a plain housewife, has nothing to recollect. In her comfortable and ideal role of wife to a rich man, Kathie has failed to acquire "things" that she can remember. She herself has not lived, and therefore her memorable possessions are very few indeed. Nevertheless, Kathie desires to have memories and what is more, she wants to see them written down, piled up, as objects with real, material existence get piled up in the closets of those who manage to possess them. While a career or a lover presupposes an unavoidable degree of interaction with the world, memories can simply be made up, organized, mixed with fantasy and desire, written down, and then passed on as a life. Kathie then decides to fantasize her memoirs, which bear no resemblance to Elena Garro's historical novel *Los recuerdos del porvenir* (1963 [*Recollections of Things to Come,* 1969]), in spite of the superficial similarity in their nomenclature. Kathie's memoirs are recorded in a space rather distant from the conventions of everyday life in a Latin American city, because rather than memories, they are actually the projection of repressed desire in conjunction with a fantasy nurtured by Hollywood's idea of the exotic, and by the sentimentality of soap operas. Kathie's quest is thus an attempt to move from her vacuous present on to an exciting, albeit invented, future, a future that bears weak, if any, logical or historical relation to her present reality.

Distantly echoing the Marquis de Sade, Kathie becomes convinced that the reality of her memory/desire would become more believable and tangible if it acquired the flesh and bones of a written text. The power of the linguistic symbolic order would thus overcome the fading, unreal mediocrity of her life. Truth would be what is written and not what is lived. Unfortunately, Kathie has been deprived not only of living and memories, but also of reading. Her writing can conjure up only nothingness itself. Her words are blank. So she decides to buy the services of a writer to write down her fantasies. She hires Santiago Zavala (Zavalita of *Conversation in The Cathedral)* to be her ghostwriter. Zavalita, a news journalist, is to write Kathie's fabulous memories of a trip to Africa. Neither the fraudulent memories of Kathie nor the writing produced by the hired Zavalita have anything in common with Isak Dinensen's biographical memories in *Out of Africa* or the brilliant surrealism of Raymond Roussell's *Impressions d'Afrique.* Kathie's fantasy and love affair with Zavalita emerge straight out of the melodramatic fantasy of Pedro Camacho the scribbler, or Sinchi, the pseudo-news journalist of *Captain Pantoja. Kathie y el hipopótamo* turns out to be yet another parody on the writer who writes that he or she writes.

Kathie y el hipopótamo, like Aunt Julia and the Scriptwriter, Who Killed Palomino Molero? and *The Real Life of Alejandro Mayta,* shares in the configuration of plots and characters, the monstrous and scatological basis of the melodrama. These texts, which in some way question what we have come to understand as metawriting, offer in fact a ludicrous and superficial solution to the problems involved in the relation of the sign and its referent. The manner in which Kathie's or Belisario's problem is cast, however, skirts both the Borgesian concept of the sign (human construct) and Derrida's problematics of meaning. Vargas Llosa's plays seem more concerned with the problem of imitation set within the dichotomy of the false/real; this dichotomy returns us to the dynamics of imitation encapsulated in the culture of the *huachafo,* and subsequently, has little to do with Borges's philosophical skepticism or Derrida's unnerving nihilism.

Mayta's Real/False Life

In *The Real Life of Alejandro Mayta* the novelist's quest comes closest to the métier of the investigative reporter. In a parallel movement the novel feeds its development through a continuous questioning of both the nature of writing and its relation to the truth. In this political novel the paradoxical and complex relation between fiction and history is of major importance. It is within the framework of the problem of writing as the representation of history that the novel's central concern with the ideological discourse has to be understood and weighed. *La historia de Mayta* engages the discourse of Christianity, Marxism, liberation theology, and the liberalism of the "Chicago Boys" as sources for action in the plot. Even though the author of the novel, the main character in the novel's making, tells us that his desire and motivation for writing is to find out what the nexus is, what secret thread binds the all-powerful Catholic orthodoxy to the militant revolutionary obscurantism,[1] the same writer repeats throughout the novel that all he wants to do is write a novel. In a novel, according to the author of the novel he is writing, "what I use is not the veracity of the testimony, but rather, the power to suggest and create color and dramatic force" (114). Such a novel has achieved its purpose when it is "an unrecognizable version of what happened" (93).

These problem-riddled relations between real events

(events lived and documented by individuals contemporary with the happenings in question) and the fabricated events of fiction also incorporate the tense and difficult relations among testimony, interview, questioning, and false testimony. Where does the truth of history lie? How to arrive at it if not by way of language and discourse? How do we ascertain the difference between a fraudulent totality and a partial truth, or an objective truth and a motivated or ideological version of the real events? Interpretation seems to be an inescapable bind for the author of *Historia de Mayta*. But, we may ask, how do we guard interpretation from the very same perils outlined above? Is interpretation not subject to the same processes of writing that allow for the colors of motivation, ideology, and fabrication? Is a fabricated image of the truth less truthful than the facts of the matter in utter disarray? Are the facts themselves not cultural constructs subject to change and revision? Such are the epistemological problems resting in the novel's undergirth. These issues tantalize the novel's discourse, but nowhere are they fully addressed. While the novel's discourse explicitly embraces the problem of truth in history and fiction, the novels' story falls short of the mark, for it constantly shifts its focus from Mayta the man, the little *cucaracha* (roach), to Mayta the marginal devotee of an amorphous and perhaps misguided homophilia, to the narrator's serious or ludicrous search for the truth understood as fictional material.

Mayta's story is the biography of a poor, sad, uncertain, strange fragile little man. Physically, morally, intellectually, and psychologically, Mayta turns out to be rather unattractive, to say the least. At most, this fat, pale little man can evoke compassion. As a revolutionary his lack of physical endowment is not compensated with a fiery intellect like Trotsky's or a strategic genius like Lenin's. Mayta is not even a shadowy reflection of the tall, strong, courageous, brilliant Fidel Castro, or of the asthmatic but indefatigable doctor and theoretician Che Guevara, or even of the Conselheiro of fierce, mystical gaze. In fact, Mayta's portrait has been drawn from the ranks of the moles and the roaches, a choice which appears more clearly in *El Hablador* with Zurata's filiation to Kafka's Gregory Samsa. It is a denial, much more than a caricature, of the romanticized revolutionary of Latin American political history.

Differing from Pantaleón, another poor soul, Mayta does not provoke laughter. His behavior and unfathomable, private goals prove irritating to the reader who must follow his expulsion from one circle into another, until he is left with no one other than his one equally strange revolutionary partner, Lieutenant Vallejos. Unlike Zavalita, Mayta is incapable of gaining the reader's empathy for his vague "revolutionary" plans. It is difficult to believe that in this stubborn but humble man we have the making of a fanatical and dangerous revolutionary. Mayta's image turns out to be amorphous, confused, easily and gratuitously contradictory. He and his project seem miscast in a possible revolutionary scenario in Peru. Mayta as historical revolutionary personage drawn from the pseudopainstaking investigation carried out by the novel's main narrator remains unconvincing, for he is too distant from the historical and novelistic mimetic conventions of the hero or the great man; he bears no resemblance to any of the real revolutionaries named above, or even the many politicians who have dotted the political landscape in Peru with their failed dreams and corrupt governments. Above all, Mayta is unconvincing because his revolutionary project is never unfolded for the reader's consideration. It is a secret, a vague hope, a senseless crisscrossing of activities that seem unjustifiable. Mayta, in fact, never had a chance in real life, nor does he get a chance in this fictional pseudobiography of the historical referent, Rentería. His final destiny is the only one he was suited for all along: ice cream man.

Autobiography/Biography and Realism

In contrast with this poor and misguided man the text erects the persona and seductive presence of the author who investigates and writes Mayta's story. This character—the writer—openly and directly addresses his readership. He establishes a direct bridge between himself as a historical person and his reader as another real person, over the fiction that he is creating for the reader implied in the pages of the fiction. In this manner Vargas Llosa breaks with one of the most sacred conventions of Flaubert's realism: indirect narration, the undetectable omnipresence of the Godlike author. In this text Vargas Llosa the author, not Marito, appears as a character in his own fiction, thus problematizing the mimetic illusion of objectivity to which he so faithfully and brilliantly had adhered in his early novels.

The character Mario Vargas Llosa, as in *Aunt Julia*, appears deployed here in two time frames. On the one hand he is the author, contemporary with the reader of the novel, who investigates and documents Mayta's story; on the other hand he appears as Mayta's schoolmate, a generational contemporary of the religious and compassionate adolescent. The character Vargas Llosa, in consonance with the autobiographical pact, is recognizable to the reader by the same individual, gender, and social marks that would designate the author Mario Vargas Llosa outside the text. This character/autobiographer is a famous and respected novelist who lives part of the year in Barranco, a suburb of Lima, and who travels the rest of the year throughout Europe and the United States. His prestige is immense, and his connections are so extensive in the official Peruvian world that all he has to say is that he needs an interview or a certain document for the doors to be immediately opened for him. Differing from Marito in *Aunt Julia,* the character of the writer is never parodied. On the contrary, the narrator's credibility rests on the notion that the narrator is one and the same with the author of the book, and that he is in turn the historical Mario Vargas Llosa. Thus, the realistic reading pact, as different from the comic reading pact, between the reader and the narrator of the story relies upon the narrator's own self-characterization as witness and historian of the events that he is about to narrate. Within this realistic frame or pact the reader is offered a series of facts already known in the narrator's consciousness, and maybe even in the memory of other readers who also happen to be generational contemporaries of Mayta's and César Vallejo's historical referents, for the events of Jauja do have an actual historical referent. For the second time Vargas

Llosa breaks an inviolable tenet of realistic conventions: he presents and relies on a contradictory narrator. The narrator in *Historia de Mayta* both possesses all the narrative might ascribed to the author Vargas Llosa and is stymied by the pettiness of facts and their ultimate lack of clear significance emanating from the combination of plot and the novel's discourse.

At the beginning of the story the writer/character implied in the narrator's voice announces that he is going to reconstruct and write the obscure and perhaps forbidden or silenced story of the unknown revolutionary Alejandro Mayta. Among other reasons, the narrator is interested in Mayta because he had been a high school friend. Thus, the novel promises to be both autobiography and biography. Soon, however, these possibilities fade out, because the writer begins to interview people who shared with Mayta experiences of much greater importance than those that a passing high school acquaintance might have shared with the revolutionary. At this point the story of the novel begins to look more like the history of a whole generation in Peruvian life. The novel's social referent, like that in *Conversation in The Cathedral,* is clearly the generation that came to maturity during the Odría dictatorship. It is generally referred to as the 1950s generation, and it encompasses intellectuals such as Vargas Llosa, Julio Cotler, Antonio Cornejo Polar, Abelardo Oquendo, Max Hernández, Oswaldo Osorio, Javier Silva Ruete, and others. As the novel progresses, the writer/character writes a story that in fact could be taken to be a version of Mayta's life. At the same time the writer/character reflects upon the vexing question of revolutionary change in Peru in relation to the political opportunities and commonsense choices available to the different groups that adhere to leftist or Marxist ideological schemes.

Parallel to this reflection upon the left's ideology, the same writer/character reconnoiters Lima in search of people who may have known Mayta, identifying and visiting places where Mayta lived or where he was imprisoned. The writer/character even travels to Jauja, a small town in the northern Andes, where Mayta forged the last stages of his aborted revolutionary plan. The writer/character takes pains to share with his reader his documentary sources, the kind of analysis or imaginary use to which he subjects them, and the reasons why he uses "sources" in the making of his fictional biography of Mayta. The writer assures his reader over and over again that he does not "intend to write the true history of Mayta." This endeavor entails, rather, the exhaustive compilation of data so that later, by adding huge doses of imagination, he may produce an unrecognizable but true version of Mayta's life. The writer makes it abundantly clear that between history and fiction, he opts for the privileges and the truth of fiction (77).

From the beginning of the story the reader is led to believe that the flatulent little Mayta, or his counterpart in history, died in one of the many failed guerrilla movements in Peru in the 1960s. But the reader is flabbergasted when, at the end of the story, the writer/character tells him that Mayta not only survived jail but is now free, and at age fifty works as an ice cream man, is happily married, and is ready to be interviewed by the writer. Only at that moment the writer/character announces that, from the start of his quest, he always meant to interview Mayta. Even though the reader could accept this late revelation and back-and-forth dialectic regarding the true/false relation between history and fiction, the fact that Mayta is now married stretches, in the face of his much scenified homosexuality, the bounds of historical mimesis, and causes the reader to wonder if Mayta's story is not another parody emanating from Camacho's pen.

Some readers have not seen the possible parodial coloration of the whole story. Readers intimately aware of the facts of guerrilla movements in Peru have read in this novel a sort of obfuscation of history in deference to fantasy and in opposition to the political activity of the left in Peru. Antonio Cornejo Polar, Peru's most influential literary critic, has written that "even if *Historia de Mayta* were to be built on the freest imagination, the novel does not exhaust itself within the universe of fiction: it represents a real consciousness [reflecting] upon situations that are also absolutely real."[2] Representing the critical reception accorded the book in many other quarters in Latin America, the Peruvian critic adds:

> Formalized in the proliferation of interrogations and conditional modes, ambiguity becomes the major symbol of the text itself. This is why, perhaps, caught in a given moment between the literary potential of "Mayta's story" and the character and social symbol attributed to his adventure, the narrator declares that "in fact, I don't know why Mayta's story intrigues and perturbs me."[3]

Speaking about the historical referent evoked and used in the novel, Cornejo shows the differences between the fictional character and the historical person on whose political adventure the story of Mayta rests. A contemporary of the historical facts fictionalized in the novel, Cornejo Polar writes that:

> *Historia de Mayta* introduces significant changes, especially in relation to the past:
> a) Rentería is substituted by Mayta, and Mayta is portrayed as a homosexual. . . .
> b) The events of Jauja are moved forward all the way to 1958, so that they become previous to the Cuban revolution, the [Peruvian] guerrilla movement of the 1960s, and the peasant uprisings of the same decade. It is therefore possible to interpret them as the "beginning of the history that has ended up in that thing that we now live." It is clear that this chronological displacement is used by the narrator in order to privilege the abortive Jauja revolt, conferring upon it an inaugural condition. . . . In this regard, it is impossible not to point out that it turns out to be a tergiversation to situate in the same line, and characterize in the same manner, the events in Jauja, with the guerrilla movement of the 1960s and the many acts of popular violence that have since then—also before then—exploded in Peru, and the Shining Path.[4]

Meaning and Narrative Structure

Even though the illusion of reading a historical or political novel does not emerge from the pages of *The Real Life of Alejandro Mayta,* the sense of reading a journalistic diary or a long report on a faraway country does mark the pages of this novel. This sense of a report is especially strong in the scenes in which the narrator visits the miserable shantytowns of Lima, the work of nuns connected with liberation theology and service to the poor, the forbidding jail where Mayta spends his prison term, and the journey to Jauja. The feeling is due in part to the fact that the narrator used almost exclusively the narrative device of the interview. Vargas Llosa's previous extensive use of conversation has been noted as one of his innovative narrative devices. The interview can be conceived as a modulation in the art of conversation. However, between his early novels and *The Real Life of Alejandro Mayta* an important difference exists. In this last novel Vargas Llosa textualizes the past (a past not yet over, a past that reaches right into the start of the narrative act) and the present (a present of the the narrator that coincides with the present of the reader) in only two temporal frames and one single story. In this novel Vargas Llosa limits the number of speakers engaged in dialogue to the conventional two. Also, he limits the time frame embraced by each of the dialogues to one. The interview either focuses on the present or evokes the past. The few times when the complex assemblage of several simultaneous conversations, as perfected in *Conversation in The Cathedral,* is used, in *The Real Life of Alejandro Mayta* it proves to be merely repetitive. Even when more than two speakers are involved, they wait to take their turn to speak; they don't switch from the present interlocutor to addressing a person involved in the evoked past scene or event, as we saw in *The Green House.* The problem of the narrator's identity, which often enriched the message of Vargas Llosa's early novels (e.g., not knowing that in *The Time of the Hero* certain melancholy and sweet interior monologues actually belonged to Jaguar) does not play a part in the narrative rhetoric of Mayta's story.

Both *The Real Life of Alejandro Mayta* and *Who Killed Palomino Molero?* are, technically speaking, minor texts in Vargas Llosa's oeuvre. In these two novels, as well as in his plays, the number of elements included in the *art combinatoire* has been reduced. The possibilities of combination are even smaller in *El hablador*. Frequent and unforeshadowed shifts in narrator, combination of points of view, mixing of physical and emotional distance from the events or the character, combination of idiosyncratic narrative styles and vocabulary, and shifts in the temporal and spatial frames of the stories, among other hallmarks of Vargas Llosa's narrative, all seem to be evolving in the stories of Mayta, Palomino, and Mascarita/Saúl Zurata. These stories are narratives organized on the basis of one single chronological line in which the narrator's investigative work or evocation is intertwined with the forward movement of the story's own chronology. In others, the story starts with a beginning that eventually but directly arrives at a denouement or ending.

In spite of the fact that the moment of the enunciation has been located at a future date, an instance not yet seen in history—the invasion of Peru by North American soldiers in the north and by Cuban and Bolivian troops in the south—the story of *The Real Life of Alejandro Mayta* moves forward slowly. The sordid events in Mayta's life seem pale by comparison with the courage, butchery, fanaticism, and technicolor inferno of *The War of the End of the world* and Camacho's truculent soaps. Mayta's story's new and fascinating development runs through at the ideological level of the novel. The action that Vargas Llosa has tried to reproduce is no longer the adventure of the body in the casting of (and the war in) Canudos, but the adventure of the mind and the person in the thorny forest of ideology. The ideological tenets, the ideological fractions, the ideological consumption and polemical disputes of the Peruvian left, are the topoi which dominate the human portrait in this political novel.

Within the framework of intellectual and ideological action Mayta, who started out being a devout Catholic, ends up being an uncompromising communist suspected of operating at the service of the CIA. Again, as in *Aunt Julia* and *The Green House,* the person's idiosyncrasy and identity seem extremely unstable categories. Mayta's transformations or switches are a little harder to believe, precisely because in his case we have more details with which to imagine the sharp differences between a devout Catholic and an uncompromising communist. Vargas Llosa's novel in fact seeks to question these differences, and to propose that between Christian brotherly love and communist solidarity there is not great gulf.

Because of either restlessness, intellectual vanity, or political stupidity, Mayta fails in everything. Like a *pícaro* he moves from group to group, from secret cell to secret cell, managing in the end to be expelled from all groups for lack of intellectual or political discipline. In the end he and Vallejos, another marginal character, get together to make their own revolution, a revolution that ultimately turns out to be as imaginary as Kathie's trip to Africa. The entire novel gives testimony to Mayta's pathetic confusion and his bottled-up despair at living in a society in which life is literally cheap, and in which change for the better seems to be an illusion. Lost in history, Mayta and his leftist *camaradas* seek refuge in the fantasy of revolutionary change, in a revolution that would seem to have little connection with the millions of lives resigned to *la vida,* as Oscar Lewis's anthropological studies of marginal life in Mexico City showed more than twenty-five years ago.

Mayta's story presents a wretched revolutionary deprived of all means of possible success. In this pessimistic story neither history nor the individual revolutionary has anything to do with glory, affirmation of the individual self, or the destiny of a nation. On the contrary, Mayta, the ice cream man, represents not only the demythification of the revolutionary (Che Guevara, Fidel Castro, Sandino, Bolívar) but also the very denial of any such image. Mayta is buried in a Kafkian alienation that brings to mind Samsa's insectlike existence in *The Metamorphosis*. Both Samsa and Mayta share a diminutive, gender-unspecific size. Both insect-men smell; they are poor, ugly, false, fidgety, and no doubt destined to fail in a humanly voracious, violent world. Finally, the major interest of this novel does not stem from its possible status as historical or experimental novel. The importance of *The Real Life of Alejandro Mayta* rests on the possibility of its being read as a text wrestling with the questions of ideology and its place in writing (*écriture)* and in the coming to pass of history.

Tasurinchi Gregorio and/or El Hablador

In his latest novel Vargas Llosa, the autobiographical narrator, tells the story of his friend Saúl Zurata. He also tells of the Machiguengas' cosmogony, their health rituals, their hallucinatory dreams, their material culture based on fishing and slash-and-burn cultivation of yucca, the origin of their moral codes, and the divine as well as material reasons for their endless peregrination through the Amazonian forests at the head of the Madre de Dios River in southeastern Peru. The text of the story begins with the author/narrator strolling on one of the narrow little streets of Florence and accidentally spotting a photographic exhibit of peoples from the Amazon Basin. A closer look reveals to Mario Vargas Llosa the fact that the people captured in the photographs are the same Machiguengas he once visited twenty years earlier. From this point on, the story leaps back in time to the author's days in San Marcos and his friendship with Saúl Zurata, a fellow student doing field research on the Machiguengas.

The novel will alternate chapters in which the author/narrator Vargas Llosa evokes his friendship with Zurata and their common interest in the Machiguengas. Each chapter set in Lima, with intercalated brief scenes set in Florence, is followed by a chapter in which an *hablador* speaks about the cosmogony, adventures, rituals, and beliefs of the Machiguengas. While the story would seem to center on the events in Lima—mainly about Zurata's sudden disappearance from Vargas Llosa's circle of friends and acquaintances—the connections between what the *hablador* speaks and Vargas Llosa's own account of his pursuit of the Machiguengas' world and story describe a subtle thematic web. In the end the two stories, like two parallel rivers coming to the same estuary, flow together, mix, and come to a single end in the revelation that the author/narrator makes about his "decision" to cast Zurata as the *hablador:* "He decidido que el hablador de la fotografía de Malfatti sea él. Pues objetivamente no tengo manera de saberlo.[5]

In *El hablador,* Vargas Llosa intertwines several stories told by two central narrators: Mario Vargas Llosa and *el hablador,* or speaker, of the Machiguenga ethnic group. Upon closer examination things are neither so simple nor so clearly cut, for in the end we find ourselves in the presence of a mystery: Is there really an *hablador,* or storyteller, among the Machiguengas? And if there is such an institution, does the voice (enunciation) of the *hablador* textualized in the novel belong to one of several Tasurinchi (men)? Or can we ascribe all the sections in which supposedly one Tasurinchi speaks to Tasurinchi Gregorio? Or is the *hablador* as a character in the novel and as a Machiguenga institution simply an invention of Mario Vargas Llosa? The answer to all these questions is yes, depending on the point in the story where we ask them, and on how much data regarding the Machiguengas or Saúl Zurata we may muster outside of the novelistic text.

If we, like most readers, have no external data on either Saúl Zurata or his historical referent, or the world of the Machiguengas, we have to conclude that the import of the plot of *El hablador* is both fictionally and historically true. The novel's logic would lead us to conclude that Zurata, the anthropologist, refused his scholarship to France and then staged his own disappearance from Lima in order to fulfill a secret and passionate desire: to become one with the Machiguenga culture he was studying. Furthermore, within this plot logic we would also have to conclude that the *hablador* "quoted" in the novel is in fact Zurata, masquerading as a Machiguenga *hablador*. But this narrative, as in previous fictions by Vargas Llosa, denies the reader key pieces of the puzzle, so that the denouement, though revelatory, also remains ambiguous. *El hablador* does not provide the reader with sufficient information in order to ascertain how, where, or even if the autobiographical narrator himself ever saw or heard Zurata/the *hablador* telling stories to the Machiguengas, or the Machiguengas in a mixed group with missionaries or anthropologists. The identity of a (any) *hablador* and Zurata remains as conjecture on the part of the autobiographical narrator. What is more, in the final pages of the novel Vargas Llosa goes one step further. Back in Florence, placing the finishing touches on *El hablador* and reminiscing about the photographic exhibit that unleashed in his imagination the bottled-up inquiry into the Machiguengas, Vargas Llosa, speaking as the author within, as well as outside, the text of the novel, tells his reader that in interpreting one of the photographs he has decided that the relatively tall standing man is Zurata. He has further decided that the shadow on one of his shoulders is the parakeet (totem) of the *hablador*. Once this act of interpretation has been completed and reported to the reader of the novel, the same reader is invited (not persuaded) to believe in the identity of Zurata as the standing man in the photograph, and as the *hablador*. In this play of masks Zurata (also known as Mascarita) becomes and embodies the enunciation of the *hablador* already profiled in the text of the novel. What we have "learned" about the Machiguengas changes substantially inasmuch as we have learned it from Zurata, masquerading as one of their *habladores,* and not from an authentic keeper of the tribe's beliefs and traditions. The change in the sign of the enunciation changes the nature of what is enunciated. Moreover, the reader must now perform one more revisionary function to the meaning of the text. It is now necessary to go back to all the places where the word *Tasurinchi* appears in combination with the *hablador* function and erase *Tasurinchi* (man, in Machiguenga). In the place left by the erasing of the common noun *Tasurinchi,* Saúl Zurata must be written in. Here the second reading begins. The novel returns its wiser reader to the beginning.

As in *The Real Life of Alejandro Mayta* and *Aunt Julia and the Scriptwriter,* in *El hablador* Mario Vargas Llosa deploys an autobiographical situation in which he, the author, engaged in investigative reporting, tries to put together the dispersed pieces of a puzzle. But the puzzle seems to have its own raison d'être, and while it yields an answer to the detective's own question, in doing so the puzzle brings up a larger problem. So that while the story seems to concentrate on Saúl Zurata's anthropology and his disappearance from Lima, the introduction of this character in the story of the Machiguengas becomes at once superfluous and crucial. Saúl Zurata's interest in the Machiguengas becomes superfluous in light of the bibliography that the "author" or narrator Vargas Llosa offers on the ethnology, cosmology, witchcraft, and language of the Machiguengas.[6] Zurata's anthropological and anthropo-philial quest is crucial to the book's own quest about the nature and function of storytelling and the capacity of one human being to literally put himself in the place of another—that is, the ability to impersonate, to pretend, and to imagine a credible self and a credible discourse within the limited bounds of a given culture. The transformation of Zurata into an *hablador,* a transformation that is not explored in the novel but is announced at the end of the story, is in fact the transformation that the reader witnesses throughout the novelistic text as he realizes that the stories told by the *hablador* are actually the discourse of Zurata turned *hablador*. In this context Zurata becomes a superfluous mask for Vargas Llosa himself, who in *El hablador* portrays at least four versions of himself as four different, though not separate, incarnations. On the one hand, Vargas Llosa portrays Vargas Llosa, the famous writer spending his vacation time in Florence, reading Dante, writing his novel, sipping cool drinks in and reminiscing about the mystery of his lost friend Saúl Zurata and his own days as a poor San Marcos undergraduate. As the writing of *El hablador* moves on, we find a Vargas Llosa among his friends in Lima, almost coerced by force of friendship and love for experimentation to create, film, and host a weekly T.V. show, *La torre de Babel* (The Tower of Babel), based on documentaries and on onsite filming in Peru and the rest of Latin America. In this incarnation Vargas Llosa makes a documentary on Pinochet, another on Doris Gibson, and yet another on the Peruvian guerrilla movements of the 60s and the dramatic killing of the young poet Javier Heraud in the Peruvian jungle. In yet another incarnation Mario Vargas Llosa portrays the part of himself that took him to the Peruvian jungle to visit with the North American missionaries of the Instituto Linguístico de la Selva, to old and forgotten sections of European libraries and convents in search of material on the Machiguengas, and most especially in search of documentation on the Machiguengas' vaguely reported institution of the *hablador*. And finally, in *El hablador,* we find the most powerful transformation of all, Vargas Llosa's own creation of the *hablador's* world, story, and discourse. In this last transformation we can see how Vargas Llosa has appropriated Zurata's most personal desire and made it his own. If Zurata ever truly wished to know the feel of the Machiguengas' sense of being, it was to be Vargas Llosa's and not Zurata's or anybody else's anthropological account that would achieve that point of credible identity between the world and the word.

Within Vargas Llosa's oeuvre appropriation and recreation of the peculiarities of class, ethnic, or national world view have been the hallmarks of his creativity. His characters have escaped the flatness of the stereotype because they possess distinct linguistic constructs of their own and therefore become memorable. Fushía's lament and self-pity, Amalia's naïve and disinterested telling of the wickedness of others, Ambrosio's reluctant voice, the Conselheiro's unmitigated condemnation of sin and sweet embrace of the repenting, are all emblematically embedded in speech acts peculiar and logical only to their persons, class, ideology, and morals. Whether it has been the social, physical, political, or moral setting for the action of his novels, Vargas Llosa has always depicted the world of his fiction through the consciousness of those who lived it, and never through the consciousness of an author capable of abstractions and aware of the consequences that his characters—in accordance with their class or position—could not fathom even though it was their destiny to live the daily exploitation, corruption, epidemics, national politics, and religious intolerance cast in the plot.

Masquerading the Machiguengas

In *El hablador,* Vargas Llosa succeeds once more in masquerading, or rather creating a convincing sensorial and ideological world for Tasurinchi, or the Machiguenga individual male. Delineating the parameters and peculiarities of the Machiguenga speech act is no doubt the greatest challenge thus far faced by Vargas Llosa's art of representation, for the Machiguenga world that his storyteller engages in cannot be readily encapsulated within the reason or the logic of the absurd known to the West. Not long ago the West considered the World of the native peoples of this hemisphere as primitive. From such characterization it followed that their culture was identified as "primitive," meaning only irrational mental processes and a simple and crude material life. Within this characterization, knowledge, as the West knew it, had not been mastered by such peoples. Anthropology, archaeology, medicine, and linguistics have taught us in the last half of this century that the cultural logic of such "primitive" peoples, while different in its peculiarities, is in fact not substantially different from the cultural logic of any other group of humans, especially those characterized as civilized. We have learned, for instance, that the empirical knowledge of the medicinal resources of the Amazon jungle is a knowledge based on thousands of years of trial and error, experience and experimentation, knowledge encapsulated in nonscientific terms but a very useful and reliable knowledge indeed. Lévi-Strauss, in his *Trïstes Tropiques* (1955), left an enormous legacy toward the understanding of the social and mythical logic of the Caduveo in Brazil. Although many dispute Lévi-Strauss's stance in relation to primitive knowledge, it is nevertheless important to remind ourselves here that, at the conclusion of his studies in Brazil, he wrote that

> the inquiries of archaeology and anthropology show that certain civilizations—some of them now vanished, others still with us—have known quite well how to solve problems with which we are still struggling. To take one instance only: it is not only a few years since we discovered the physical and physiological principles on which are based the Eskimos' customs and manner of life. If they can exist in these conditions, it is not from long conditioning, or from an exceptional physical constitution, but from their discovery of scientific principles of which we had until lately no idea. So true was this, that it also exploded the pretensions of those explorers who had claimed to have "improved upon" Eskimo costume: the results were the opposite of those that had been hoped for.[7]

In another sector of recent inquiry, myth studies have shown that the art of storytelling of ancient civilizations (Greece, Judea, India) and the so-called primitive (Machiguenga, Caduveo, Chontal), and for that matter the "moderns," does not essentially differ inasmuch as all myths attempt to tell stories by which the absurdity of death, illness, crime, and transgression can be understood and assimilated as part of a reason that explains the world as it is. Moreover, myth is not the fossilized reason of the primitive past. In fact, the mythical dimension remains alive in almost all storytelling or narrative structures.

In *El hablador,* Vargas Llosa unfolds and displays the reason and the reasoning of the Machiguenga people, the reason that gives coherence to their myths. Such a reason or discourse explains the origin of the world, the location of the moon in the sky, the reason for the moon's spots, the reason behind the taboos observed by the Machiguengas, the origin of disease, the status of totems, and above all the cosmological as well as historical reasons for Machiguenga errantry. Each story told by the *hablador* conjugates cosmogonic, historic, and environmental factors in the making of the plot. For the Machiguengas the material world of their habitat is filled with signals that indicate to them the presence of evil little devils setting about to bring illness or hunger upon the family group, and nature's indication that its ability to support further human habitation has been exhausted. In the *hablador's* discourse, in the stories he tells to his spellbound listeners, the divine is inextricable from the human, and these in turn appear as one with the minute workings of the jungle environment. The Machinguengas believe, for instance, that it is their duty as civilized men to move from site to site in the jungle because in this constant errantry they help support the sun's rising and setting. If they were to settle forever in a given site, the sun might never recover from its last setting. However, they are also keenly aware of the fact that they move around the jungle to avoid contact with the *viracochas* (the Peruvians, Brazilians, Bolivians, or North Americans), who from time to time appear in the jungle in search of Machiguengas for their labor camps or their missionary endeavors. The fear of contact with the white *viracochas* is based on the empirical observation that these people bring deadly disease. There is nothing more frightening to a Machiguenga than a *viracocha* sneezing. The Machiguengas' recollection of the time of the bleeding of the trees (the rubber boom) is alive with the terror of disease, hunger, separation from their people, exploitation, and premature death. Their ancient solution was to "get going," to obey the old tradition of their people and move on farther into the unknown recesses of the jungle, even into places where yucca cultivation, fishing, and hunting seemed impracticable. Each isolated little family settled once more near a *caño* (river branch), cleared a patch of earth, planted the yucca, set traps, observed the prohibitions, and fulfilled its destiny: not to disappear from the face of the earth. From time to time they rejoiced in the visit of the storyteller. This Tasurinchi's destiny is to live alone, to be forever on the go, to visit the scattered Machiguenga family groups, and to hold long sessions with the herb doctors. The *hablador* is the man who, for all intents and purposes, keeps the ethnic group's identity and continuity alive in time and space. He brings gossip, and he tells about the origins of people, the jealousy and envy of the gods, the mythical and empirical origin of disease, the many available cures, the symptoms of disease, and above all the place where the souls of those who "leave" (die) go in order to return once more in the form of animals or new human beings. The *hablador* is the vehicle by which the memory of the Machiguengas binds them together as a collective. Memory feeds solidarity of spirit and purpose. The tales of the *hablador,* the myths of the Machiguengas, inasmuch as these embody their collective experience and their sense of each other as part of a commonly shared daily life and reason for living, both express and mold the Machiguengas' sense of self and world view.

The above is the abstracted anthropological summary of the contents of the many tales that the Tasurinchi created by Vargas Llosa deploys in his own narrative strategy. In the text of Tasurinchi, time has only a before and an after: places are up or down river; dreams and hallucination erase the division between consciousness and reverie. In this world all men are simply known as Tasurinchi, and all women are a Tasurinchi's daughter, wife, or mother. Tasurinchi's level of self-awareness is, however, highly developed. He often questions himself as a narrator, reflects on the veracity of his stories. Almost all his stories close with "that is how it happened. Perhaps." Tasurinchi not only aspires to be a spellbinding storyteller; he would like to achieve wisdom, for he believes that there is a reason for everything. Everything has an explanation. Wondering about the reason for the death of his three sons, the herb man reflects:

> "That has an explanation," says the herb man. "Everything has one. The man-hunting during the time of the tree-bleeding has one, too. But it is hard to find out. Not even the *seripigari* can always find out. Maybe the three of them went to talk, over there, with the mothers of this place. With three dead here, the mothers will not see us as strangers here. We are from this place now. Don't these trees and birds know us? Don't the water and the air of this place know us? Perhaps that is the explanation. Since they left, we have not felt animosity. It is as if they had accepted us, here" (137).

And so the Tasurinchi listens, he travels wide and far in search of the empirical knowledge of the herb doctor, in search of the knowledge devised in the *mareadas* or hallucinations under the influence of *masato* or *ayahuasca*. But wisdom, the Tasurinchi learns, is a hard thing to come by; even the herb doctor agrees on this judgment. Tired of the *hablador's* inquiry into the origin of the animals, the *seripigari*, or sage, tells the *hablador* to stop asking questions:

> They were all somewhat different from what they are today. They all must have gone through something worth telling. Would you like to know their stories? Me too. Many of the ones I know I learned from the *seripigari* at Kompiroshiato.... But one day, he threw me out of his house. "How long are you going to stay, Tasurinchi?" he said, scolding me. "You have to leave. You are an *hablador,* I am *seripigari,* and now, so many questions, making me talk so much, you are changing me into what you are. Would you like to become a *seripigari?* You will have to be born again. Pass all the tests. Purify your-

self, have hallucinations, and above all, suffer. It is hard to achieve wisdom" (189–90).

This search for wisdom, a search embarked on by means of storytelling, a search that is given at once in the story told as well as the telling of the story, is in fact the quest of the entire novel. While in *Conversation in The Cathedral* Santiago's quest for knowledge takes him past the gates of hell to a place in which all hope has to be abandoned, in *El hablador* the quest for wisdom takes Vargas Llosa and Zurata to the world and the historical consciousness of the Machiguengas, people who have taken the most extraordinary measures to keep themselves separate and uncontaminated from the destructive ways of other men. Machiguenga wisdom holds that the Machiguengas must at all costs stay away from all other cultures, assimilate not one iota of other men's beliefs or ways. They must abstain from all the sinful foods, and in order to remain pure, the prohibitions must be flawlessly observed. One man asks another, "What must one do in order to remain serene, Tasurinchi?" The answer is, "Eat what is prescribed and respect the prohibitions, *hablador*" (185).

But at another level of discourse in the novel it is the Machiguengas' inextricable relationship to cultural and biological purity in relation to survival in historical identity that articulates the central issue of the novel and the central issue in Peruvian history from the Spanish invasion of the Andes to the present. In the autobiographical sections of the novel Vargas Llosa reproduces his discussions and differences with Zurata on the question of assimilation of the Machiguengas and other Amazonian natives to the economy and history of Peru. Zurata, the student of the Machiguengas and of the history of Peru, inasmuch as it is the history of the destruction or assimilation of native culture to the West, argues that no greater harm can be done to any people than the wholesale destruction brought on by civilization, or rather the expansion of the West. The autobiographical narrator, openly identified with Vargas Llosa the historical figure, questions Zurata's thesis and even ridicules it by saying that his position of "leave them alone" is not only impractical, but that it resembles Valcárcel's early indigenist position in relation to the Andean peoples (Quechua and Aymara) of Peru. The paradox of the novel is that even though Vargas Llosa doubts the wisdom and truthfulness of Zurata's position, the novel itself builds a test case in which the culture of the Machiguengas referred to as primitive by Vargas Llosa himself emerges as a self-sufficient, highly civilized, and enduring human construct. Thus, the "civilizing" pretensions of the Instituto Linguístico de la Selva, other missionary groups, or even anthropologists or the Peruvian state seem not only unnecessary but also self-serving.

What remains outstanding in the argument is the inevitability of contact and the equally inevitable process of acculturation. By proposing the story of Zurata's transformation into the *hablador,* Vargas Llosa vitiates the entire argument on behalf of the cultural self-sufficiency of the Machiguengas. Since the *hablador* is in fictional fact Zurata, and Zurata is a modern, trained anthropologist, it would follow that no authentic *hablador* could have rendered the Machiguenga memory and discourse in as orderly or fascinating a narrative as Zurata/the *hablador* does in the pages of *El hablador*. In fact, Vargas Llosa's missionary informers—Catholic and Protestant—tell him, when he asks about the *habladores,* that these men tell a bunch of boring, inchoate stories about the stars and the moon. Edwin Schneil, the Protestant missionary who reports a vague encounter with an *hablador,* tells Vargas Llosa that the fellow

> talked, talked without stopping, without pause, or period. Just like all *habladores* speak. Telling about all manner of things. What a chaos. [He spoke] of everything that came into his head, . . . of the four worlds of the Machiguengas, of his travels, of the magical herbs, . . . of celestial geography, of the labyrinth of rivers with impossible names (177, 171).

Nowhere in the text of *el hablador* is there any direct presentation of the anthropological data, the literal recording of an informer's stories, of the speech act of any *hablador.* In Peru extensive anthropological work has been done, collecting the myths of the Amazonian people. The Amazonian Center for Anthropology and Practical Applications has published in various journals the results of work with Amazonian informants.[8] What is more, Machiguengas questioned by Vargas Llosa deny the existence of any such person or function within their group. The autobiographical narrator conjectures, at the end of the novel, that this is so because the Machiguengas are protecting the identity and even the existence of Zurata, their spokesman. This would lead us to suspect that Machiguengas, in fact, have no such memory, no such myths, and that their entire discourse is the result of, or the creation of, an anthropologist turned Machiguenga. From here one can put into question the very assertion regarding the self-sufficiency of the Machiguenga culture, and what is more, one can conclude that their survival as a separate and "pure" culture depends on the unlikely possibility that "other" men will make the decision to join the Machiguengas and become men of the forest themselves. It is this point where the fictional fact of Zurata's Jewishness comes to play an important function in the discourse of the novel. The Machiguengas wander the jungle in search of ethnic and cultural purity. When faced with contact with other peoples, they assimilate a few individuals as their own and then move on, in order to avoid further contact with impurity and collective annihilation. But, can or should the Machiguengas repeat Jewish history, given their number and the state of their culture in relation to the predatory culture of the *viracochas*; or is Zurata's transformation only an isolated example of the capability of one individual to become, to impersonate, the desired self? The fact that Vargas Llosa, in a Cortazian gesture worthy of the writerly problematics of *Blow-Up,* tells that he has *decided* to make of the man in the photograph the figure of Zurata would seem to remove the consequences of the novel's discourse from the realm of history and claim for it a purely fictional, fabricated status. Nevertheless, the cultural problems embedded in the discourse of the novel—the ongoing polemic between Indigenists and Hispanics in Peru—remain short of any possible intellectual resolution.

Given the history of Latin America, however, and the quest of many Latin American writers to come to grips with the mosaic of peoples and cultural traditions that the continent harbors, one cannot fail to recognize that *El hablador* continues the tradition established by Miguel Angel Asturias, Alejo Carpentier, and José María Arguedas. These three master writers set out to reconstruct their own experience with the non-Western heritage of the history and lives of their fellow countrymen in a novelistic form capable of rendering the world of the Maya, Quechua, and Caribbean peoples into a coherent and believable whole. With *El hablador,* Mario Vargas Llosa joins the anthropological aspiration and practice of many of the most celebrated Latin American writers. In creating a verisimilar language for the *hablador*'s enunciation and world, Vargas Llosa has inaugurated a new, almost lyrical style absent in his previous work. While avoiding the baroque lexical and sentence formation of Asturias in *Mulata de Tal* (1963 [*Mulata,* 1967]) or Carpentier's so-called magic realism, Vargas Llosa's prose for the *hablador* comes closer to Arguedas's subtle management of Spanish linguistic structures in the exploration of a sense of the divine in natural and human affairs. With *El hablador,* Vargas Llosa continues the exploration of the autobiographical novelistic mode in a crisp journalistic prose and places right next to it, and in yet a new juxtaposition, a clean and pared style for mythic narrative. And yet his previous emphasis on the scatological functions of the body, his rendition of scenery as part of the speaker's consciousness of sensorial perception, remain as clear marks of the narrative oeuvre of the author of *The War of the End of the World.*

NOTES

1. Mario Vargas Llosa, *Historia de Mayta,* (Barcelona: Seix Barral, 1984) 120. Translations are mine; page numbers are given in parentheses.

2. Antonio Cornejo Polar, "La historia como apocalipsis," *Quéhacer* 33 (1985) 79–80.

3. Cornejo Polar 53.

4. Cornejo Polar 68, 79–80.

5. Mario Vargas Llosa, *El hablador,* (Barcelona: Seix Barral, 1987) 230. All translations are mine. "I have decided to make him the speaker in Malfatti's photograph. And this is so because there is no way for me to know objectively."

6. See *El hablador* for the references given in the novel as possible sources for ethnographic data on the Machiguengas. As of this writing, I have not been able to check on Father Joaquín Barrales, or the anthropologist Johnston Allen, or the Swiss ethnologist Gerhard Baer. But since Vargas Llosa has lately shown a greater fascination with Borges, scholars must check for themselves the quality of the bibliography mentioned in a given fictional text.

7. Claude Lévi-Strauss, *Tristes Tropiques, and Anthropological Study of Primitive Societies in Brazil,* trans. John Russell (New York: Athenium, 1968) 383.

8. In *Antologia general de la prosa en el Perú; 1895–1985,* vol. III, ed. Luis Millones (Lima: EDUBANCO, 1986), Enrique Ballón writes a short introduction to the selections included in this volume from the jungle ethno-literature of Peru. Citing the work of Manuel García-Rendueles and the Centro Amazónico de Antropología y Aplicación Práctica, the prologue clearly establishes the differences between the oral myth, or *mito vivido,* and its degraded rendition into written language. García-Rendueles writes: "We want to present, not our interpretation of the myth or a global understanding of the narrative, but rather the myth itself exactly as it was narrated, with all its tedious repetitions, its desinhibited language, and also how the group perceived the myth." For a full bibliography on the Machiguenga see Esther Espinosa/Alejandro Camino, "Bibliografia Machiguenga" in *Amazonía Peruana,* vol. VI, no. 11, 1987, pp. 161–81.

CONCLUSION

Nearly thirty years have elapsed since Vargas Llosa erupted into the world of Latin American and international letters with his dazzling *The Time of the Hero.* In more than a dozen works of fiction he expanded his narrative world from the circumscribed space of the Leoncio Prado Military Academy to the vast back lands of the northeastern interior of Brazil and the Amazon Basin. In each of his works he has met new technical challenges in narrative as well as in the complexity of the world that his pen was to capture and portray. Moreover, the artist has wrestled publicly and openly with the possibility of creating for himself an aesthetic capable of critically justifying, if not explaining, his own work and its evolution from the socially committed novel to the satire of the victims of a racist and obscurantist system. In his *El hablador,* he makes very plain what his unflinching commitment to writing fiction has meant for him: storytelling is also a valid, perhaps an essential and primordial way of seeking, and maybe reaching, knowledge about the world we experience and create. While he has forcefully argued for the *desinteresado* (unmotivated) character of a true and good novel, in his later works, *The Real Life of Alejandro Mayta* and *El hablador,* he has posited an autobiographical narrator engaged in the ideological polemics of the political right and left in Latin America. In *El hablador* it would seem that Vargas Llosa questions seriously the good that can result from social change, especially from the massive social change involved in the imposition of a new system, as well as the social change which advocates of the poor and marginal pursue. And yet, deciding not to emulate the Machiavelli that he reads as he writes *El hablador,* deciding not to draw any "glacial lessons" from *The Prince* in managing the polity, Vargas Llosa prefers to close his reflection on the good of civilizing or progressive enterprises on a cautious and guarded note:

> After having turned them around several times, after attempting several possible combinations, the pieces of the puzzle come together. They delineate a more or less coherent story, upon condition of not delving beyond the anecdote, upon condition of not asking oneself questions about what Fray Luis de León called "the very own and hidden principle of all things" (*El hablador,* 230–31).

Ironically, and "upon condition of not delving beyond the anecdote," it would seem that Vargas Llosa's ideology of writing has come full circle. Having started out as a committed writer, in what he believed was a Sartrean existentialist position, and having later repudiated Sartre's claim to the unavoidable engagement of fiction, in favor of a Flaubertian cannibalism of reality as the mere materials in the making of autonomous fictional worlds, Vargas Llosa deploys in his later novels a narrator involved in direct and polemic political discourse. While *Captain Pantoja and the Special Service,* as well as *Aunt Julia and the Scriptwriter,* coming as they did after Vargas Llosa's public break with the Cuban revolution, laugh unhibitedly at some of the most painful realities of the continent, the subsequent appearance of *The Real Life of Alejandro Mayta* and *El hablador,* attest to the fact that even when the "author" in the novel makes himself a corresponding object of satire and ambiguity, the calamities of Latin American history continue to impose the weight of their intractability upon the writer of fiction.

The strategy of the detective novel so deftly used in *Conversation in the Cathedral* seems insufficient before the complexity of the historical problems implied as well as inscribed in *El hablador* or *The Real Life of Alejandro Mayta*. If the pieces of the puzzle come together at the level of the anecdote, the very fit of Zurata's or Mayta's journey seems exhausted and disconcerting at the level of the deep structure. If the telling of stories, as Lévi-Strauss proposes, is an immanent category of the mind, then we must recall that telling stories or mythmaking has remained a timeless human activity because stories organize and thus give meaning to experience. As Freud and Lévi-Strauss have shown, the deep grammar of dreams and myth sign the mysteries of life into significant wholes.

In fictionalizing, that is in the course of giving form and meaning to previously unrelated and even contradictory signs, Vargas Llosa has created a powerful picture of a socio-symbolic universe caught in a constant process of decay. He has often recognized this remarkable quality of his own imaginary. What is more, he has claimed it to be the indispensable faculty of the novelist—a man in constant search for materials in state of decomposition. His most successful metaphors for the novelist's métier have established a symmetry between "cannibalization," "orgiastic rituals," "decomposition," "fire," "deicide," "strip-tease" and the novelist's conjugation between writing and his imaginary.

In keeping with this portrait of the novelist that Vargas Llosa believes he has been, his texts have crossed many heretofore forbidden frontiers of the Latin American bourgeois imagination and the Catholic Church. With *The Time of the Hero, Captain Pantoja* and *The War of the End of the World,* Vargas Llosa tore off the heroic mask of the military in Latin America. In novel after novel, the writer has gone beyond the self-serving portrayals of different sectors and institutions of Spanish American society. He has dismantled the notion that the upper sectors of semi-educated gentlemen and ladies are gifted with a class sense of noblesse-oblige. Correspondingly, he has also chosen to portray the poor and oppressed in a sordid war against one another. Finally, he has challenged and mocked the self-appointed monopoly on the truth which the politicians and social-scientists of the left have claimed for themselves in Latin America. This wholesale dismantling has left very little standing in the place of the former verities. The writer, before the smoldering ruins wrought by the demons of his pugnacious inquiry, like the Barão de Canhabrava after the holocaust of Canudos, indulges in a little *divertimento.* A text to pass the time, *Elogio de la madrasta,* 1988, (In Praise of the Step-Mother) is his most recently published novel.

Elogio de la madrasta is already a best-seller. Lavishly illustrated in full color, the slow porno-erotic novelette makes easy and even perhaps forbidden reading. Each scene, heavily focused on the female body as object of fantasy and desire, reiterates the commonplaces of foreplay with a body presented in a sequence of atomized pieces and moments. To Vargas

Llosa watchers, the publication of *Elogio de la madrasta,* subtitled "the vertical smile," and containing the story of the seven-year-old Ponchito's seduction of his stepmother, seemed either the ultimate act of defiance, or proof that Vargas Llosa the novelist was not really seriously interested in running in the forthcoming presidential elections in Peru.

Nevertheless, events in the arena of Peruvian politics have defied the expertise of the pundits. The last twenty years have witnessed in Peru the rise of Liberation Theology alongside the growth of the Shining Path guerrilla movement. Neither governments of the moderate left nor administrations by the old right have been able to stem the perceived disintegration of the *ancien-regime*. Somehow the key pieces of the puzzle have thus far proven elusive.

Vargas Llosa has always been a keen observer of political developments in the governing of Peru. In the last ten years he has participated strongly in the political debate engaged by all contending sectors of the Peruvian polity. More and more he has been identified with the forces of former president Fernando Belaúnde's conservative faction of Acción Popular. Vargas Llosa is now actively campaigning as the presidential candidate of the right in the national elections to take place in 1990.

SELECT BIBLIOGRAPHY

Works by Mario Vargas Llosa

Fiction

Los cachorros. Pichula Cuéllar. Barcelona: Editorial Lumen, 1967.

La casa verde. Barcelona: Seix Barral, 1965.

La ciudad y los perros. Barcelona: Seix Barral, 1963.

Conversación en La Catedral. Barcelona: Seix Barral, 1969.

La guerra del fin del mundo. Barcelona: Seix Barral, 1981.

Elogio de la madrastra. Madrid: Tusquets, 1988.

El hablador. Barcelona: Seix Barral, 1987.

Historia de Mayta. Barcelona: Seix Barral, 1984.

Los jefes. Los cachorros. Barcelona: Seix Barral, 1980. Contains "El desafío," "Los jefes," "El abuelo," "Día domingo," "El hermano mayor," and "Un visitante."

Pantaleón y las visitadoras. Barcelona: Seix Barral, 1973.

¿Quién mató a Palomino Molero? Barcelona: Seix Barral, 1986.

La tía Julia y el escribidor. Barcelona: Seix Barral, 1977.

Fiction, English Translations

Aunt Julia and the Scriptwriter. Trans. Helen R. Lane. New York: Farrar, Straus, 1982.

Captain Pantoja and the Special Service. Trans. Ronald Christ and Gregory Kolovakos. New York: Harper & Row, 1978.

Conversation in The Cathedral. Trans. Gregory Rabassa. New York: Harper & Row, 1975.

The Cubs and Other Stories. Trans. Gregory Kolovakos and Ronald Christ. New York: Harper & Row, 1979. Includes translations of stories in *Los jefes.*

The Green House. Trans. Gregory Rabassa. New York: Harper & Row, 1968.
The Real Life of Alejandro Mayta. Trans. Alfred Mac Adam. New York: Farrar, Straus, 1986.
The Storyteller. Trans. Helen Lane. New York: Farrar, Straus, 1989.
The Time of the Hero. Trans. Lysander Kemp. New York: Grove, 1966.
The War of the End of the World. Trans. Helen Lane. New York: Farrar, Straus, 1984.
Who Killed Palomino Molero? Trans. Alfred Mac Adam. New York: Farrar, Straus, 1987.

Literary Criticism and Journalism

"Carta de batalla por *Tirant lo Blanc.*" Preface to Joanot Martorell, *Tirant lo Blanc.* Madrid: Alianza, 1969.
Contra viento y marea. Barcelona: Seix Barral, 1983.
Entre Sartre y Camus. Río Piedras: Huracán, 1981.
"La experiencia de los novelistas." Interview with José Miguel Oviedo. *Revista Iberoamericana* 48 (Jul.-Dec. 1981).
García Márquez: Historia de un deicidio. Barcelona: Barral, 1971.
García Márquez y la problemática de la novela. With Angel Rama. Buenos Aires: Corregidor/Marcha, 1973.
Historia secreta de una novela. Barcelona: Tusquets, 1971.
José María Arguedas, entre sapos y halcones. Madrid: Ediciones Cultura Hispánica del Centro Iberoamericano de Cooperación, 1978.
"La literatura es fuego." *Mundo Nuevo* 11 (1967):93–95.
"Martorell y el 'elemento añadido' en *Tirant lo Blanc.*" Preface to Martín de Riquer and Mario Vargas Llosa, *El combate imaginario: Las cartas de batalla de Joanot Martorell.* Barcelona: Barral, 1972.
La novela. Montevideo, 1966.
La novela en América Latina: Diálogo. Literary discussions

with Gabriel García Márquez. Lima: Carlos Milla Batres, 1968.

La orgía perpétua: Flaubert and Madame Bovary. Madrid: Seix Barral, 1975.

"Sebastián Salazar Bondy y la vocación del escritor en el Perú." Preface to Salazar Bondy, *Obras completas*. Lima: Moncloa, 1967.

Criticism and Journalism, English Translations

"A Fish Out of Water." *Granta* 36 (Summer 1991): 15–77.

"The Genesis and Evolution of *Pantaleón y las visitadoras*." Ed. and trans. Raquel Chang-Rodríquez and Gabriella de Beer. New York: The City College of New York, 1977.

"The Latin American Novel Today." *Books Abroad* 44 (1970):41–45.

"Literature Is Fire." *Doors and Mirrors*. Ed. Hortense Carpentier and Janet Brof. New York: Grossman, 1972, 430–35.

"A Media Stereotype." *Atlantic* Feb. 1984:20, 22, 24.

The Perpetual Orgy. Trans. Helen Lane. New York: Farrar, Straus, 1986.

"Social Commitment and the Latin American Writer." *World Literature Today* 52 (1978):6–14.

"Updating Karl Popper." *PMLA* 105 (1990):1018–25.

"The Writer in Latin America." *Index on Censorship* 7 (Nov.-Dec. 1978):34–40.

A Writer's Reality. Ed. Myron I. Lichblau. Syracuse: Syracuse University Press, 1991.

Drama and Film

Kathie y el hipopótamo: Comedia en dos actos. Barcelona: Seix Barral, 1983.

Pantaleón y las visitadoras. Film. Paramount Pictures, 1976. Script and direction: Mario Vargas Llosa and José María Gutiérrez.

La señorita de Tacna: Pieza en dos actos. Barcelona: Seix Barral, 1981.

Works about Vargas Llosa

Books

Antología Mínima de Mario Vargas Llosa. Buenos Aires: Editorial Tiempo Contemporáneo, 1969.

Asedios a la realidad: Mario Vargas Llosa. Las Palmas: Inventarios Provisionales, 1972.

Boldori de Baldussi, Rosa. *Vargas Llosa: Un narrador y sus demonios*. Buenos Aires: Fernando García Cambeiro, 1974.

Cano Gaviria, Ricardo. *El buitre y el ave fénix: Conversaciones con Mario Vargas Llosa*. Barcelona: Anagrama, 1972.

Castro-Klarén, Sara. *Mario Vargas Llosa: Análisis introductorio*. Lima: Latinoamericana Editores, 1988.

Oscar Collazos, *Literatura en la revolución y revolución en la literatura: Polémica*. México: Siglo XXI, 1970.

Diez, Luis A. *Mario Vargas Llosa's Pursuit of the Total Novel. A Study of Style and Technique in Relation to Moral Intention*. Cuernavaca: CIDOC, 1970.

———, ed. *Asedios a Vargas Llosa*. Santiago: Editorial Universitaria, 1972.

Fernández, Casto M. *Aproximación formal a la novelística de Vargas Llosa*. Madrid: Editorial Nacional, 1977.

Geisdorfer Feal, Rosemary. *Novel Lives: The Fictional Autobiographies of Guillermo Cabrera Infante and Mario Vargas Llosa*. Chapel Hill: University of North Carolina Department of Romance Languages, 1986.

Gerdes, Dick. *Mario Vargas Llosa*. Boston: Twayne, 1985.

Giacoman, Helmy F., and José Míguel Oviedo, eds. *Homenaje a Mario Vargas Llosa*. Madrid: Las Américas, 1972.

Lewis, Marvin A. *From Lima to Leticia*. New York: University Press of America, 1983.

Luchting, Wolfgang A. *Mario Vargas Llosa: Desarticulador de realidades*. Bogotá: Andes, 1978.

Martín, José L. *La narrativa de Vargas Llosa: Acercamiento estilístico*. Madrid: Gredos, 1974.

Oviedo, José Miguel. *Mario Vargas Llosa: La invención de una realidad*. Barcelona: Barral Editores, 1970; Editorial Seix Barral, 1982.

———, ed. *Mario Vargas Llosa*. Madrid: Taurus, 1981.

Pereira, Armando. *La concepción literaria de Mario Vargas Llosa*. México: Universidad Nacional Autónoma de México, 1981.

Rossman, Charles, and Alan Warren Friedman, eds. *Mario Vargas Llosa: A Collection of Critical Essays*. Austin: University of Texas Press, 1978.

Williams, Raymond Leslie. *Mario Vargas Llosa*. New York: Ungar, 1986.

Special Journal Issues

"Focus on *Conversation in The Cathedral*." *Review* 14 (1975).

"Homenaje a Mario Vargas Llosa." *Norte* 12 (Oct.-Dec. 1971).

"An Issue Devoted to the Work of Mario Vargas Llosa." *Texas Studies in Literature and Language* 19 (1977).

"Literature as Fire: The Achievement of Mario Vargas Llosa." *World Literature Today* 52 (1978).

Articles

Brody, Robert. "Mario Vargas Llosa and the Totalization Impulse." *Texas Studies in Literature and Language* 19 (1977): 514–21.

Castro-Klarén, Sara. "Fragmentation and Alienation in *La Casa verde*." *Modern Language Notes* (March 1972):286–99.

———. "Humor and Class in *Pantaleón y las visitadoras*." *The Latin American Literary Review* (Fall-Winter 1978):64–79.

———. "Dolor y locura: la elaboración de la historia en *Os Sertões y La guerra del fin del mundo.*" Special issue of *Revista de Crítica Latinoamericana* (Fall 1984):207–30.

———. "Santos and Cangaceiros: Inscription without Discourse in *Os Sertões* and *La guerra del fin del mundo.*" *Modern Language Notes* (1986):366–88.

Coleman, Alexander. "The Transfiguration of the Chivalric Novel." *World Literature Today* 52 (1978):24–30.

Cornejo Polar. "La historia como apocalipsis." *Quéhcer* 33 (1985):79–80.

Filer, Malva E. "Vargas Llosa, the Novelist as a Critic." *Texas Studies in Language and Literature* 19 (1977):503–13.

Foster, David W. "Consideraciones estructurales sobre *La casa verde.*" *Norte* 12 (1971):128–36.

Franco, Jean. "Conversations and Confessions: Self and Character in *The Fall* and *Conversation in The Cathedral.*" *Texas Studies in Literature and Language* 19 (1977):452–68.

Fuentes, Carlos. "El afán totalizante de Vargas Llosa." in *La nueva novela latinoamericana.* México: Joaquín Mortiz, 1969, 35–48.

Hudelson, Richard. "On Mario Vargas Llosa on Truth and Freedom." *PMLA* 106 (1991):534–35.

Mayer, Enrique. "Peru in Deep Trouble: Mario Vargas Llosa's 'Inquest in the Andes' Reexamined." *Cultural Anthropology* 6 no. 4 (1991).

Moody, Michael. "The Web of Defeat: A Thematic View of Characterization in Mario Vargas Llosa's *La Casa Verde.*" *Hispania* 59 (1976):11–23.

Morello-Frosch, Marta. "Of Heroes and Martyrs: The Grotesque in *Pantaleón y las visitadoras.*" *Latin American Literary Review* (Spring-Summer 1979).

Prieto, René. "The Two Narrative Voices in Mario Vargas Llosa's *Aunt Julia and the Scriptwriter.*" *Latin American Review* 11 (1983):15–25.

INDEX

"abuelo, El," 21–22
Acción Popular, 228
African Queen, The, 62
Aguaruna, 43–44, 49–50, 55, 60, 65, 145
Aída, 84, 99, 101
Alberto/the Poet, 21, 23, 28–31, 33, 35–38, 58, 144, 156
"Aleph, The" (Borges), 121
Amado, Jorge, 54
Amalia, 80, 86–92, 97–98, 101, 105, 211
Amat, Oquendo de, 3, 128
Amazon, 20, 46, 53–55, 62, 138, 140, 145, 206, 212, 224
Amazonian Center for Anthropology and Practical Applications, 220
Ambrosio Pardo, 79–81, 86–97, 101, 156, 211
Annual Critic's Award (Argentina, 1980), 16
Anselmo/the Harpist, 38, 45–48, 51–53, 58, 69, 75
Antología Mínima de Mario Vargas Llosa (Poniatowska), 42, 117;
  Antonia, 46–48
Antonioni, Michelangelo, 190
Aprista party, 88
Aquilino, 12, 47–48, 51, 54, 71–74
Arequipa, 87, 93, 95–97, 99, 187
Arguedas, José María, 3–4, 117, 222
armas secretas, Las (Cortázar), 190
Asturias, Miguel Angel, 222
Aunt Julia and the Scriptwriter (La tía Julia y el Escribidor), 15–16,
  86, 118, 139, 148–60, 163–65, 172, 175, 185, 189, 192, 196–97, 204,
  209, 225
Aunt Julia, 15, 86, 136, 149, 150, 151, 155, 156, 157
ayahuasca, 217

"babas del diablo, Las" (Cortázar), 190. See also *Blow-Up*
Bahia, 164, 166, 170–71, 179, 181, 185–86
Bakhtin, Mikhail, 117, 118
Balzac, Honoré de, 20, 115
Barão de Canhabrava, 169, 170–72, 182, 185–86, 227

Barão de Gerembão, 171. *See also* Barão de Canhabrava
Barthes, Roland, 81, 114
Bataille, George, 116
Beatito, 174–76
Beauvoir, Simone de, 115
Becerrita, 86, 98, 101, 103
Beckett, Samuel, 116
Being and Nothingness (Sartre), 5
Belisario, 190, 192
Bellavista, 22, 26
Blow-Up (Antonioni), 190, 221
Boa, 22, 27–30
"bodas de Camacho, Las" *(Don Quixote)*, 159
Bogart, Humphrey (in *The African Queen*), 62
Bonifacia/La Selvática, 12, 38, 44–45, 47–51, 55, 58, 63, 75, 144, 175
Borges, Jorge Luis, 1, 121, 132, 152, 192–93
Borgnine, Ernest (in *McHale's Navy*), 14
Brando, Marlon (in *Tea House of the August Moon*), 14
Brazil, 2, 16, 54, 71, 95, 163–64, 166, 178, 181, 186, 224
Breton, Restif de la, 7
Brother of the Arch (Crisanto Maravillas), 156, 158, 187
Brotherhood of the Arch, 139, 142, 144
Buscón (Quevedo), 159
Butor, Michel, 116

cachorros, Los. See *Cubs and Other Stories, The*
Caduveo, 213–14. See *Tristes Tropiques*
Cahuide group, 84, 144
Camacho (Pedro), 15, 139, 149, 151–57, 159, 161, 166, 172, 190, 192, 200, 203
Camus, Albert, 115–17, 126
cangaceiros, 181, 183
"cannibalizing," 118
Cano Gaviria, Ricardo, 117, 146
Canto de sirena (Martínez), 89
Canudos, 17, 166–71, 173–74, 180, 182–86, 204, 227
caño, 215
Captain Pantoja and the Special Service (Pantaleón y las visitadoras), 13–15, 136, 139–49, 163–65, 187, 192, 225, 227

Caracas, 40, 122, 124, 133
Carlitos, 86, 98, 102–4
Carmesina (in *Tirant lo Blanc*), 68–69
Carpentier, Alejo, 43–44, 63, 222
"Carta de batalla por *Tirant lo Blanc*," 125
Casa Verde, La. See *Green House, The*
Castro, Fidel, 164, 195, 205
Catedral, The, 80–81
Cathedral, The, 81
Catholic Church, 110, 227
Cava, 23, 30, 35
Cayo Bermúdez, 85, 86–94, 98–101, 139
Celine, Louis Ferdinand, 78
Centurion, The, 17. *See also* Hollywood
Cervantes, Miguel de, 8, 107–9
Champs, the, 47–48, 50, 144
"Chinese boxes," 68, 70, 95
Chispas, 82–83
cholo, 137
Christianity, 64, 187, 193
Circle, The, 11, 23, 26, 36, 144
ciudad y los perros, La. See *Time of the Hero, The*
Comercio, El (Lima), 21
Commander of Streets, 174. *See also* Conselheiro (Antonio)
"communicating vessels," 68, 70
Conrad, Joseph, 78
Conselheiro (Antonio), 17, 164, 166, 169, 170–71, 174–82, 195, 211
Conversación en La Catedral. See *Conversation in The Cathedral*
Conversation in The Cathedral (Conversación en La Catedral), 12–13, 77–106, 117, 127, 144, 149, 165, 187, 192, 198, 202, 218, 226
Conway, Tim (in *McHale's Navy*), 14
Cornejo Polar, Antonio, 198, 200
Cortázar, Julio, 1, 114, 190, 221
costumbrismo, 123
Counselor. *See* Conselheiro (Antonio)
criollo, 137–38, 142, 145
Cuban revolution, 2, 40, 42, 125, 164, 201, 225
Cubs and Other Stories, The (Los Cachorros; *with selections from* Los jefes), 19, 21, 77–78

Da Cunha, Euclides, 16, 163–64, 166, 169, 171–73, 176, 182, 184
Dante Alighieri, 105–6, 210
Derrida, Jacques, 192–93
"desafío, El," 9, 22
Dialogic Imagination, The (Bakhtin), 117
Dickens, Charles, 58
Diez, Luis A., 68–69, 163, 192
Dinesen, Isak, 192
"Día Domingo," 22
Don Fermín Zavala/Bola de Oro, 73–74, 83–84, 86, 88–91, 94–95, 99, 102–3
Don Quixote (Cervantes), 107, 110, 148, 159
Doña Bárbara (Gallegos), 4, 41
Doña Zoila, 83–84, 86, 98
Dos Passos, John, 78
Dostoyevsky, Fedor, 78
Dumas, Alexander, 7, 45, 47

El buitre y el ave fénix: Conversaciones con Vargas Llosa (Cano Gaviria), 117
Elianita, 157–58
Elogio de la madrasta (In Praise of the Step-Mother), 227–28
Emma (in *Madame Bovary*), 132
Emperatriz (in *Tirant lo Blanc*), 107
Entre Sartre y Camus (Between Sartre and Camus), 126–28
Existentialism, 5–6
Exodus, 16. *See also* Hollywood
écriture, 205

Father García, 47, 53
Faulkner, William, 8, 78, 153
"feeding on carcasses," 118
Fitzcarraldo (Herzog), 63
Flaubert, Gustave, 2, 7, 108, 115–16, 118–20, 123, 125, 129–31, 136, 196, 225
Flies, The (Sartre), 6
Florence, 206, 208, 210
Ford, Glenn (in *Tea House of the August Moon*), 14

Fracción Universitaria Comunista Cahuide, 123. *See also* Cahuide group
French New Novel, 115
Freud, Sigmund, 226
Fuente Benavides, Rafael de la (pseud. Martín Adán), 3
Fuentes, Carlos, 1
Fushía, 12, 44, 47–48, 51, 53–54, 56, 58, 63, 71–75, 95, 144, 211

Galileo Gall, 169–72, 185–86
Gallegos, Romulo, 4
Gamboa (Lieutenant), 137, 142
García Márquez, Gabriel, 1, 116, 128–30, 136
García Márquez y la problemática de la novela (edited with Angel Rama), 117
García Márquez, historia de un deicidio, 13, 128
Garro, Elena, 191
Geisdorfer Feal, Rosemary, 159
Gerdes, Dick, 53, 58, 67, 78
Gibson, Doris, 210
Gilligan's Island, 14
Golden Toes, 36, 144
Gonçalvez Viana, 171, 185
Greece, 214
Green House, The (La Casa Verde), 6, 11–13, 19–20, 38, 40–76, 77, 95, 99–100, 108, 122–23, 144–46, 163–64, 175, 202, 204
Gregory Samsa (in *The Metamorphosis*), 195, 205
guerra del fin del mundo, La. See *War of the End of the World, The*
Guerra, Rui, 163–64
Guevara, Ernesto (Che), 195, 205
Guillén, Claudio, 159
Guzmán de Alfarache (Alemán), 159

hablador, 205–6, 208–11, 214, 216–20
hablador, El (*The Storyteller*), 20, 118, 145, 172, 188, 195, 203, 206–22, 218, 224–26
Hasta no verte Jesús Mío (Poniatowska), 42
Hemingway, Ernest, 8, 49, 78, 116
Hepburn, Katharine (in *The African Queen*), 62

Heraud, Javier, 117, 211
"hermano menor, El," 22
Hero's Dwelling, The (La morada del héroe; *intended title for* The Time of the Hero), 10
Herzog, Werner, 63
Higueras, 26, 38
Hipólito (in *Tirant lo Blanc*), 108
Hipólito, 99, 101
Historia de Mayta. See *Real Life of Alejandro Mayta, The*
Historia secreta de una novela, 13, 46, 122–23, 129
Historias de amor, de locura y de muerte (Quiroga), 44
Hollywood, 16, 166, 191
Holocaust, 55
Honorio Villanova, 168, 184, 186
Hopscotch (Rayuela), 190. *See also* Cortázar, Julio
huachafo, 137–39, 146–48, 152, 192
Huambisa, 54, 56, 145
Hugo, Victor, 7, 115
Huis clos (Sartre). See *No Exit*

Impressions d'Afrique (Roussell), 192
Inconquistables, the, 44
indigenismo, 44
Instituto Linguístico de la Selva, 211, 218
"insurrección permanente, Una," 124
Iquitos, 14, 54, 56, 73–74, 142

Jacobo, 84, 99, 101
Jaguar, 23, 26–31, 36–38, 58, 144, 203
James, Henry, 117
Jauja, 18, 197, 199, 201
Jay, Martin, 120
"jefes, Los" (in *Los jefes and Los Cachorros*), 21, 22. See also *Cubs and Other Stories, The*
jefes, Los, 19, 21. See also *Cubs and Other Stories, The*
Jesus Christ, 17, 176, 178, 180
João Abade, 167, 174, 182
João Grande, 167–68, 173–74, 182
Journal de Noticias, O (in *The War of the End of the World*), 169

Joyce, James, 78, 153
Juana Baura, 47–48, 52
Jum, 44, 47, 50–51, 55–56, 71, 75, 145
Jungle Book, The (Kipling), 44
jungle, 19, 46–47, 54, 56, 62–63, 145. *See also* Machiguenga
Jurema, 170

Kafka, Franz, 195, 205
Kant, Immanuel, 97
Kathie y el hipopótamo (Kathie and the Hippopotamus), 17, 190–92
Kathie, 190–92, 204
Kipling, Rudyard, 44
Kompiroshiato, 217

L'Etre et le néant (Sartre). See *Being and Nothingness*
L'idiot de la famille (Sartre), 125, 130
La Chunga, 47, 51, 53
La Crónica (In *Conversation in The Cathedral*), 86, 103
La Musa/Hortensia, 80, 86, 88–89, 91, 94, 98, 100–105, 144
Lalita, 47–48, 50–51, 54, 56, 75, 156
"Las bodas sordas y el sueño de Placerdemivida" (in *Tirant lo Blanc*), 68
Lawrence, D. H., 78
Lazarillo de Tormes, El, 159–60
Lenin, Vladimir Ilyich, 195
Leoncio Prado Military Academy, 3, 10, 12, 23, 43, 224
León de Natuba, 172, 174–76
Lévi-Strauss, Claude, 97, 213, 226
Liberation Theology, 228
Lima, 2, 5, 7, 12, 14, 19, 21, 51, 86–89, 91, 106, 150–51, 155, 158, 197, 206, 208–10
Literatura en la revolución y revolución en la literatura (*edited with* Collazos, Oscar), 117
"literatura es fuego, La." *See* "Literature Is Fire"
"Literature Is Fire," 3, 40–42
Lituma/The Sergeant, 38, 45, 47–48, 50–51, 60–63, 65–67, 75, 144, 156
Lo que Varguitas no dijo (Urquidi), 161
Lolita, 158
Lombardi Perry, Francisco, 165

Lost Steps, The (Carpentier), 44, 63
Ludovico, 96–97, 99, 101
lumpen, 139, 166–67, 179

Machiavelli, Niccolo, 225
Machiguenga, 145, 206–12, 214–21
Madame Bovary (Flaubert), 118, 121–23, 131
Mandrake, the Magician, 45
Mangachería, 50, 52
Marcha (Montevideo), 2
mareadas, 217
Maria Quadrado, 167, 173–76, 182
Mariátegui, José Carlos, 3
Mario Vargas Llosa's Pursuit of the Total Novel (Diez), 68–70
Marito (author), 9
Marito, 15, 86, 149–60, 164, 190, 196–97
Martín Adán. *See* Fuentes Benavides, Rafael de la
Martínez, Gregorio, 89
Martorell, Joanot, 68, 107–8, 110, 112
Marxism and Totality, the Adventures of a Concept, from Lukács to Habermas (Jay), 120
Marxism, 5, 84, 120, 193, 199
masato, 217
Mayta (Alejandro), 18, 172, 189, 194–200, 202–5, 226
McHale's Navy, 14
Mercurio Peruano, El (Lima), 21
Merlin the Magician, 112
Metamorphosis, The (Kafka), 205
Miraflores (Lima), 22, 77, 149
mise-en-scène, 189
Monde, Le (Paris), 2
Monte Santo, 175–77, 111
Moreira César (General), 169, 172, 184
Moro, César, 3, 128, 133–34
Mouches, Les (Sartre). See *No Exit*
Mulata (Asturias), 222
Mulata de Tal (Asturias). See *Mulata*

New novel, the, 8
Nieves, 50, 51, 65, 67
No Exit (Sartre), 6, 125
noche de Tlatelolco, La (Poniatowska), 42
nouveau roman, 8, 114–15
novela de la tierra. See Regionalist novel
novela, La, 111, 122–23, 125
nueva novela, 115

"objective and subjective levels of reality," 68
Odría dictatorship, 13, 79, 93, 98, 198
Odría, General Manuel, 3, 85, 99
One Hundred Years of Solitude (García Márquez), 121, 129
Oquendo, Abelardo, 198
Orgía perpetua, Flaubert y Madame Bovary, La. See *Perpetual Orgy, Flaubert and Madame Bovary*
Ortega, Julio, 67, 104
Os Sertões (Rebellion in the Backlands), 16, 163, 169–71, 176, 180, 184–85
Out of Africa (Dinesen), 192
Oviedo, José Miguel, 67, 98

Pablito, 156
País, El (Madrid), 2
Pajeú, 168, 173, 185–86
Palomino Molero, 19, 203
Panamericana Radio Station (in *Aunt Julia and the Scriptwriter*), 150
Pantaleón Pantoja (Captain), 14, 136–42, 146, 195
Pantaleón y las visitadoras. See *Captain Pantoja and the Special Service*
Paraíso en el Nuevo Mundo, El (Rodríguez de León Pinelo), 46
Paris, 5, 8–10, 46, 114–15, 157
pasos perdidos, Los (Carpentier). See *Lost Steps, The*
Patricia Llosa, 157–58
Pedrão, 168, 173, 182
Pedro de Urdemalas (Cervantes), 159
Periquillo Sarmiento, 160

Perpetual Orgy, Flaubert and Madame Bovary, The (La orgía perpetua: Flaubert y Madame Bovary), 2, 7, 115–16, 130–31
Piura, 2, 19, 43–45, 47, 50–53
pícaro, 160, 204
Placerdemivida (in *Tirant lo Blanc*), 69, 107
Pluto, 29
Pochita, 137, 140, 142, 147
Ponchito, 228
Poniatowska, Elena, 42–44, 117
Pons, María Antonieta, 14
Porras Barrenechea, Raúl, 9, 187
Porthos (in *The Three Musketeers*), 45, 58
Pour un nouveau roman (Robbe-Grillet), 8
Premio Biblioteca Breve (1963), 10–11
Premio de la Crítica (1966), 40
Premio Nacional de Novela (1967), 40
Prince, The (Machiavelli), 225
Proust, Marcel, 153
Pucallpa, 14, 87, 89

Qu'est-ce-que la littérature? See *What is Literature?*
"qualitative jumps," 68
Quechua, 218, 222
Queta, 86, 88, 92, 94, 101, 103–4, 144
¿Quién mató a Palomino Molero? See *Who Killed Palomino Molero?*
Quiroga, Horacio, 44
Quo Vadis?, 17. *See also* Hollywood

Radio Central (in *Aunt Julia and the Scriptwriter*), 151, 154–55
Radio-Television Française, 8
Rama, Angel, 117
Raskolnikov (in *Crime and Punishment*), 173
Rayuela (Cortázar). See *Hopscotch*
Real Life of Alejandro Mayta, The (Historia de Mayta), 17, 79, 145, 172, 188–90, 192–205, 209, 224–26
Reátegui (Julio), 47–48, 54–56, 58, 73–74
Rebellion in the Backlands (da Cunha). See *Os Sertões*
Recollections of Things to Come (Garro), 191

recuerdos del porvenir, Los (Garro). See *Recollections of Things to Come*
Regionalist novel, 4
Rentería, 196, 201
Reposada (in *Tirant lo Blanc*), 107
Reprieve, The (Sartre), 6, 79, 125
Revue Française Prize (1958), 9
Richi/Slave, 23, 30–31, 36–38, 103
Rio de Janeiro, 166
Riquer, Martín de, 112
Ritz Paris Hemingway Prize (1985), 166
Rivera, José Eustasio, 4, 44
Ríos profundos, Los (Arguedas), 4
Robbe-Grillet, Alain, 8, 114–16
Rodríguez de León Pinelo, Antonio, 46
roman á clef, 18. See also *Real Life of Alejandro Mayta, The*
Roussell, Raymond, 192
Rómulo Gallegos Prize (Caracas, 1967), 41, 133
"ruinas circulares, Las" (Borges), 152

S/Z (Barthes), 81
Sade, Marquis de, 191
Salambo (Flaubert), 123
Salazar Bondy, Sebastián, 3, 117, 122, 124, 128, 133
Salomón, Raul, 161. *See* Camacho (Pedro)
San Marcos University, 2–3, 9, 82, 84, 149, 206, 210
Sandinista revolution, 2
Sandino, Augusto, 205
Santa María de Nieva, 44–46, 48, 50, 55–56, 73
Santiago Zavala/Zavalita, 12, 17, 78–85, 87, 90, 92–96, 98–104, 144–45, 156, 192, 195
Sarita Huanca, 156, 158
Sartre, Jean-Paul, 5–7, 34, 79, 103, 115–17, 119–20, 123–28, 130, 225
Saúl Zurata, 172, 195, 203, 206–10, 218, 220–21, 226
"Sebastián Salazar Bondy y la vocación del escritor en el Perú," 124
Sentimental Education (Flaubert), 123
Señorita de Tacna, La (The Young Lady from Tacna), 16, 189–90
seripigari, 217

sertão, 164, 171, 177–82, 185
Shining Path, 201, 228
Sinchi, 142, 156, 192
Sister Angélica, 63–64, 66–67
Sister Patrocinio, 60–63
Situations (Sartre), 125
Spanish Golden Age, 109–10, 159
Special Visiting Service, 146
Storyteller, The. See *hablador, El*
sursis, Le (Sartre). See *Reprieve, The*

Tasurinchi Gregorio, 206–7
Tasurinchi, 207, 212, 215–18
Tea House of the August Moon, 14
Tellado, Corin, 152
"temporal distortions," 68
Terras do sem fim (Amado). See *Violent Land, The*
Three Musketeers, The (Dumas), 17, 45, 184
Tierra de Caléndula (Martínez), 89
Time of the Hero, The (La ciudad y los perros), 7, 11–12, 21–39, 60, 66, 77, 102–3, 105, 112, 124, 133, 137, 142, 144, 149, 159, 163, 165, 189, 202, 224, 227
Tirant (in *Tirant lo Blanc),* 68
Tirant lo Blanc (Martorell), 8, 13, 68–70, 107–8, 110–11, 113, 116
tía Julia y el escribidor, La. See *Aunt Julia and the Scriptwriter*
Toñita, 48, 51–53, 69
torre de Babel, La (in *El hablador*), 210
"totalization," 120
Trifulcio, 91, 96, 99, 101
Tristes Tropiques (Lévi-Strauss), 213
trompe l'oeil, 65
Trotsky, Leon, 195

Uãuà, 170
"Una insurrección permanente," 41
Urquidi, Julia, 9, 157, 161, 165

Vaeth, Joseph A., 110–11
Valcarcel, Luis E., 218

Vallejo, César, 3, 197
Varguitas, 157, 159. *See also* Marito
Vassa Barris (river), 168, 182
Vega, Garcilaso de la (Inca), 3
Vega, Lope de, 109
"verifiable reality," 111
vida y milagros de Pedro Camacho, La (The Life and Miracles of Pedro Camacho; intended title for *Aunt Julia and the Scriptwriter*), 159
Villanova Brothers, 184, 186
Violent Land, The (Amado), 54
viracochas, 215, 221
"visitante, Un," 22
vorágine, La (Rivera). See *Vortex, The*
Vortex, The (Rivera), 4, 44, 54
Vuelta (México), 2

Wall, The (Sartre), 123
War and Peace (Tolstoy), 17, 184
War of the End of the World, The (La guerra del fin del mundo), 2, 16–17, 20, 79, 145, 163–88, 203, 222, 227
What Is Literature? (Sartre), 6, 123–24
Who Killed Palomino Molero? (¿Quién mató a Palomino Molero?), 19, 173, 188, 192, 203